And We Are

CHANGED

And We Are
CHANGED

PRISCILLA SHIRER

And We Are CHANGED

ENCOUNTERS
WITH A
TRANSFORMING GOD

MOODY PUBLISHERS
Chicago

Produced with the assistance of The Livingstone Corporation
(www.LivingstoneCorp.com). Project staff includes Paige Drygas, Mary Ann Lackland,
Neil Wilson, Mary Horner Collins, Kirk Luttrell, Ashley Taylor, Susan Barton, and
Cheryl Blum.

Interior design by Cheryl Blum.

Library of Congress Cataloging-in-Publication Data
Shirer, Priscilla Evans
    And we are changed : encounters with a transforming God / Priscilla Shirer.
       p. cm.
    ISBN 0-8024-3311-1
1. Christian life–Meditations. I. Title.
BV4501.3.S54 2003
248.4—dc21

2003007134

1 3 5 7 9 10 8 6 4 2

Printed in the United States of America

FOR ANTHONY

For living a life of unbridled devotion to God

For stepping out and away from the crowd

For being different

For never acquiescing

For using your talents for Him and Him alone

For not straddling the fence

For leaving the cocoon of mediocrity behind

For living radically and outlandishly for God

For determining in your heart that He is all you need

For passionately pursuing holiness

For tolerating the jokes of your peers

For accepting the fact that you won't fit in with every crowd

For not caring what they say

For taking the ridicule of many with a shrug and a smile

For the grin on your face that tells of your secret place with the Master

For being a trailblazer, a mentor to my son . . . your first nephew

Never lose your individuality

Never accept being status quo

Never look back

Press on

CONTENTS

A SPECIAL WORD OF THANKS

To Elsa and the entire Moody Publishers staff. Thank you for helping me to convey the message of my heart to women all over the world. I am honored to work with you and am so grateful that you have partnered with me on this project.

To my new girlfriends, Paige and Mary Ann. I am in awe of your ability to take my scrambled thoughts and unedited manuscript and maneuver words in such a way that it makes sense to the reader. Thank you for spending so much time getting to know me and the message that I wanted to share in this book. I am so blessed to have worked with you on this project. Thank you for using your incredible gift for the kingdom of God.

To Miss Anne. Many years ago I asked the Lord to send a godly woman to me who could help to guide me as I find my way in ministry and in life. The Lord has answered my prayer in you. You are my friend and spiritual mentor. Your walk with the Savior inspires me to re-evaluate my own. Thank you for challenging me to go deeper, reminding me to stay focused, and taking the time to help this young woman find her way. I am honored to have your written words as the foreword to this book.

To Mom and Dad. I love you and appreciate your support and encouragement in ministry. Thank you for giving me life and entrusting me to the Lord's guidance at such an early age. These written pages are a testament to the type of parenting that I was so blessed to have. Thank you.

To the two men in my life, Jerry and baby Jackson. I cannot begin to describe how overwhelmed I feel when I think about the treasure that I have in you. There is nowhere that I would rather be than at home with you. There is no other company that I would like to keep more than yours. And there is no honor greater than sharing my life with you. Thank you for loving me, accepting me, laughing with me, crying with me, and most of all, calling me wife and mom. You are my family and always my first ministry.

FOREWORD

Priscilla Evans Shirer is a joy! Her proclamation of God's Word, her pursuit of Christ, and her passion for God's people ensure that those who hear her speak or who read her words will be blessed! She possesses the rare gift of presenting the deep things of God with warmth and humor, captivating her audiences and readers.

I first encountered Priscilla five years ago at a large convention, briefly exchanging words with her in the lobby of the hotel. In those few moments, we bonded unexplainably. Maybe the bonding was due to the fact that she is the same age as my youngest daughter. Maybe it's due to the fact that we both have well-known fathers who are outstanding preachers. Maybe it's because we both recognize that God has placed His hand on us as women, calling us into ministry.

Regardless of the reason for the special attachment that exists between Priscilla and me, it is there, and I thank God for it. I consider her to be a daughter to me in the ministry and am honored to recommend this book to you. My prayer is that as you read it, you will have a life-changing encounter with the living God, breaking out of apathy, complacency, and religiosity as you enter into the freedom of a transformed life.

Anne Graham Lotz

ONE DAY several months ago, before my husband left for work, he stopped at the bedside where I was still tucked underneath the covers and gave me a kiss good-bye. He said that he had an invitation to some type of luncheon that day and asked me to attend with him. I had nothing planned that day, so I agreed to go. I'm not one to turn down free food! My husband only knew for certain that the luncheon had something to do with the opening of a new movie. I was less intrigued by the nature of the event than by the prospect of having a delightful lunch with my husband. Little did I know what the day held for me.

I arrived at the Mansion Hotel in Dallas a little before noon and went inside to find seats. Immediately I was struck by the awesome beauty, not only of the exquisite room but also of the extraordinary decorations for the luncheon. For this event, the room had been transformed into the rain forests of Ecuador. Huge palm branches on the tables served as place mats, and tall plants were centerpieces. All around the room were enormous plants and huge, black-and-white photographs of people I didn't recognize. This event was growing more and more intriguing by the moment.

As we took our seats, I looked at the materials at each person's seat. One of the items was a replica of an issue of *Life* from 1956. Inside was an article that recounted the brutal killings of five missionaries who had gone to evangelize the Auca Indians in Ecuador. The most famous of the missionaries was Jim Elliot. I had heard of Jim Elliot all of my life, and his and his wife, Elisabeth's, ministry had always been an immense blessing to me. Now here I was sitting at an intimate luncheon to discuss the making of the movie about this historic event.

The luncheon was absolutely incredible. Although those who provided the luncheon did so with the intent of raising money to help fund a feature film about the men's story, I was the one who left spiritually richer. A man named Steve Saint, the host of the luncheon, told us that his father, Nate Saint, was one of the missionaries who died that fateful day of January 8, 1956. Steve was a young child when his father was martyred for the cause of Christ in Ecuador. Nate, Jim, and several others had tried for some time to make peace with the savage Auca Indians, and when they thought they had built a strong enough relationship to make physical contact, they flew in and camped near the Auca village. Although the missionaries were encouraged by the initial visits with the Aucas, events took a terrible turn. An Auca war party attacked the camp by surprise, and all five missionaries were speared to death. Steve Saint, now a grown man, stood before us and told us how proud he was of his father's willingness to serve the Lord, even though it cost him his very life. Steve made it clear that although he missed his father sorely, he was proud to have a legacy of a daddy who was willing to lay down everything to serve the Lord. He declared that he would rather have a father who died serving Christ than one who was still living but had no knowledge of Christ.

At this point, Steve called to the stage an Indian man known simply as "Grandfather." This primitive Auca Indian walked to the stage and draped his arm around Steve's shoulders. Steve wrapped his arm around Grandfather's shoulders. They stood side by side, enveloped in each other's arms as if they were the best of friends. Grandfather began to speak to us in his native language. Steve provided the English words to translate what this man, clad in his native garb, was saying to us. Grandfather looked at us intently and said something that left us breathless. "I am one of the men who killed Jim, Nate, and his friends that day in 1956. But since that time, I have come to follow God's carvings. We have learned His markings now, and we follow His trails."

If someone told us they had changed would we believe them?

My heart skipped a beat as I realized the magnitude of what he had said. This man had killed the messengers of God, and now here he was standing before us, embracing the son of his victim to tell us that he was a changed man! Together these two men were working to tell the story of how God had worked and is still working all things together for His ultimate good. The tears welled up in my eyes and in the eyes of those around me to see this simple man and his newfound love for the Lord. God had taken the self-described "savage" and, through His grace, had changed his and his fellow tribesmen's hearts. The missionaries who willingly surrendered all for the sake of Christ fifty years ago never knew the ripple effect that has taken place in the jungles of Ecuador.

Grandfather said that he and his tribe had heard of the massacre that took place at Littleton, Colorado's Columbine High School on April 20, 1999. His tribe had heard of how those young boys had brutally killed their fellow students. He said that when he and his fellow tribesmen heard this news they commented, "We used to be savages like that too before we came to know Jesus. We too killed each other and had no regard for human life until we came to follow Him!"

Grandfather continued by saying that a group of American students had once come to Ecuador to do a story on the savage Auca Indians. After the students had spent some time with them, one student had a quizzical expression on his face. He stood back and asked, "Where are the savages that we are supposed to be doing this story on?" Grandfather had to convince the young man that they were indeed the savages that the young people had come to see. The students were amazed that the Indians were not anything like what they had expected. They were no longer killing each other and living in a state of chaos. Grandfather expressed to us how unsettling it was to him that these students were amazed at their transformed lives.

Isn't that what the power of God is supposed to do—transform your life? These students came from a culture that has so much theol-

We need to pray for those who have no regard for human life.

17

ogy, so many churches, and so many Christian radio stations and book-stores. They have easy access to many manuscripts of the Bible and more Christian conferences than one person could ever attend. Yet these American students revealed their lack of understanding of a crucial truth: *The power of God should transform a life!*

The Bible clearly states that it is possible to be "always learning but never able to acknowledge the truth" (2 Timothy 3:7). What good are Christian programs, seminars, and institutions if those who partici-pate in them are not radically transformed by them? I fear that one of the downfalls of our highly advanced society is that we have become too educated and astute to recognize that we have not reached the knowl-edge of the Truth. And that Truth is that Jesus' death means more than just your salvation and privilege to enter into eternity. It also means that the same power that raised Jesus is available to enable you to live a victorious Christian life while you are here in history!

Those students had to go to the "savage" Indians of Ecuador to be reminded of what the power of God is supposed to look like when it radically infiltrates and changes someone's life. And on this sunny day in Dallas, at one of the wealthiest hotels in the city, an Auca man with no education and no material wealth stood before a group of well-to-do Americans. As we ate our finely catered lobster lunch, he basically said to us, "*You* are the savages. We know Jesus, and we have been changed!"

That day, I sat next to young and old, wealthy and poor, white, black, and everything in between, yet we all cried the same tears of conviction. We were all challenged by the Holy Spirit, and we realized that indeed we were the savages. When we took a close look at ourselves, we saw that we look too similar to the world and its standards. Sometimes we are so busy imitating the world that we are missing out on God's call for us to "come out from them and be separate" (2 Corinthians 6:17).

When we meet Jesus, we should change. We are not supposed to act the same anymore. There should be a distinct difference in us after coming face-to-face with the Almighty Savior. Our priorities, our mind-set, and our lifestyle as a whole should be noticeably different now that we have a new Master.

Your co-workers should notice the difference.

Your neighbor's children should notice the difference.

Your unsaved spouse should notice the difference.

Your family members should notice the difference.

Your students should notice.

Your clients should notice.

Strangers should notice!

All humankind should know that there is something different about you. You shouldn't be just like everyone else. You should no longer fit comfortably into the mold of this world. You are no longer a savage. You should be a little peculiar. There should be some things that you have to let go of, with the hope and certainty that even though you can't see the end product, God's picture and His plan are bigger and greater than anything you could ever imagine. These changes will only come about if you and I get our minds off of what we want and fill them with what He wants for us. That is not always easy, my friend, but it is worth it, because that is where we find true freedom.

The Holy Spirit's soothing yet convicting voice has begun to challenge me over the past year of my life. He has called me by name and commanded me to be all that the Father expects of me. I can no longer acquiesce to the standards set by the masses or measure my progress in holiness by what I see in others, but only by the standards set by the Word of God.

The metamorphosis of a caterpillar is one of the most beautiful and dramatic transformations in nature. The Lord longs to transform each of us from the common caterpillar into the beautiful and unique butterflies that He intended for us to be. What liberty I have found in moving my fears aside and bursting forth, full flight, wings spread, into His will for my life!

After all that Jesus did for us on Calvary and as a result of what He continues to do on our behalf daily, we must not simply be encouraged, inspired, comforted, or motivated by His Word to us. We must be set free—boldly unshackled and unashamed. For all the world to see, we must be *changed!*

Changed By His Grace,
Priscilla Shirer

We say we must be changed.
How can we be changed when we really don't know ourselves?
Why does God let us see others more than ourselves?

The Encounter That Leads to

TRANSFORMATION

John 12

CHAPTER ONE

Preparing
for an Encounter
WITH GOD

Prepared me to open my heart to do as you say.

Six days before the Passover, Jesus arrived at Bethany, where Lazarus lived, whom Jesus had raised from the dead.

John 12:1

AFTER A PERSON ENCOUNTERS GOD, she should be changed. His very presence should produce a foundational transformation in the life of the one who has met with Him. It is not enough for us to talk about what we have experienced. We should be living it out flamboyantly. This is what He expects of us. He has said in His Word, "Come out from them and be separate" (2 Corinthians 6:17). This is His call to us—to be changed as a result of our meetings with Him. But what does that change look like?

In John 12, Jesus pays a visit to His close friends sisters Mary and Martha and their brother, Lazarus. Jesus decided to share some time

with these beloved friends six days before the Passover Feast cele-
bration. He might have wanted to visit them for several reasons. Realizing
that His trials and subsequent conviction and crucifixion would soon
take place, He may have wanted to spend time with His close friends
before He died. Also, Bethany was a place of quiet rest for Jesus where
He could escape from the demanding crowds for a while. At Passover,
multitudes of people would be coming to see Him and vying for His
attention. However, John 12:1 emphasizes what I imagine was His main
reason for His visit to His friends. I am sure He wanted to inspect their
lives, because this is "where Lazarus lived, whom Jesus had raised from
the dead." The last time He had visited them, Jesus had performed a
radical miracle in their midst. God Himself had shown up, and He had raised Lazarus from the dead! An encounter like that should have changed them forever.

The Lord is also watching us to see if we are any different after we have an encounter with Him.

Mary, Martha, and Lazarus, as well as many other onlookers, had been privy to an astounding demonstration of Jesus' power and love for them, and now He had come back to visit. What would He find when He saw them next? Had His miracle altered their everyday lives? I believe Jesus was watching carefully to see how their lives had been changed and whether they were different as a result of what had happened during His previous visit. I believe that the Lord is also watching us to see if we are any different after we have an encounter with Him. I wonder if He is watch-ing you right now to see whether this will be just another book that you read and you go away the same or if this time you will be forever changed.

Steven Curtis Chapman is one of my favorite Christian recording

*when God heals us from an illness, do we learn
anything from that sickness period? Or do we go
back to old habits?*

24

artists. Not only is his musical talent incredible, but his lifestyle is also consistent with his message. I appreciate many of his songs, but my favorite is a song about the radical differences that should characterize a Christian's life. It is called "The Change." The song talks about how transformation is a choice. It's a lifestyle that boldly broadcasts to the world, "I am changed." Who cares about all the Christian paraphernalia we own and wear if we don't have the lifestyle to back it up? Why wear Christian t-shirts if our hearts underneath are not sold out for Christ? What difference does a Christian bumper sticker make if the person driving is as angry and bitter as everyone else on the road? What good is our Christianity if we are not different while here on earth? There should be some tangible, genuine evidence of a transformation. And when you and I encounter Jesus and recognize His hand moving in our lives, we should experience this radical change!

Our Primary Calling

Our life's calling is to be different, to be changed. When you and I encounter His hand moving in our lives, there should be some physical evidence of His manifest presence. God's presence always brings about a transformation.

One of the most familiar pictures of the miracle of transformation in nature is a caterpillar. And if a caterpillar does have a life calling, what do you think it is? Well, it's certainly not to remain a caterpillar! The caterpillar's ultimate reason for living is to eventually become a butterfly. In preparing to write this book, I researched the process of metamorphosis—how a caterpillar changes or is metamorphosed into a beautiful butterfly. It's fascinating to learn how the caterpillar spends its life feeding; the more it consumes, the larger it grows. Each time it molts, or sheds its skin, it grows even larger until it is mature enough to begin to spin silk into a cocoon. A caterpillar may do many things in its lifetime—eating, molting, and learning to spin silk. However, all of that activity is for one central purpose: to prepare to spread its wings one day and fly.

The Bible teaches that our primary calling in life is fellowship with God. "God, who has called you into fellowship with his Son Jesus Christ our Lord, is faithful" (1 Corinthians 1:9). You were created for the express purpose of living a life that is pleasing to and brings glory to God. Therefore, nothing you do that is not in line with that mission will bring you satisfaction, fulfillment, or freedom in this life. Even Jesus Himself knew this, and while He was here on earth, He neglected to do certain "good" things if they were not in direct keeping with His Father's specific instructions. We may play a number of different roles throughout the day—from caring for elderly parents, to balancing our children's after-school schedules, to meeting our spouse's needs and supervising a staff at work. However, those are all secondary callings. Our primary calling in life is a love relationship with Jesus. God is calling you to focus on your primary calling. Encountering Him. Experiencing His presence in your life. Knowing Him. Falling more and more in love with Him. And when we do this, we can't help but be changed.

> *Our primary calling in life is fellowship with God.*

Preparing Our Hearts

We don't have to invite God to encounter us; He is at work in our lives all the time. Showing His power. Showering us with grace. Sharing His love. The question is whether or not we'll open our eyes and recognize our encounters with Him. Many of us float through life and encounter God at different places, yet we are completely unaware of the miracle of His presence. It is only those who open their eyes and recognize the encounter with God who truly benefit from these everyday occurrences and know what it's like to be changed.

What is their secret, the key to a transformed life? How do some bold believers pursue Christ with such passion that they receive the fullness of all that God is offering them in each encounter? I have discovered that it starts with preparation. People who encounter the Lord are those who take time to prepare their hearts to recognize and benefit from an encounter with God. We must cultivate our contact with Him on a daily basis in order to recognize His hand in an encounter. If we really want to change, we must seek God first, turn our attention to Him, and show Him we are serious about our relationship with Him. Mary and Martha had prepared themselves to encounter the Master. They were ready to receive from Him and experience true transformation.

> Now a man named Lazarus was sick. He was from Bethany, the village of Mary and her sister Martha. This Mary, whose brother Lazarus now lay sick, was the same one who poured perfume on the Lord and wiped his feet with her hair. So the sisters sent word to Jesus, "Lord, the one you love is sick."
>
> When he heard this, Jesus said, "This sickness will not end in death. No, it is for God's glory so that God's Son may be glorified through it." Jesus loved Martha and her sister and Lazarus. Yet when he heard that Lazarus was sick, he stayed where he was two more days.
>
> John 11:1–6

Lazarus had become sick, and Mary and Martha had sent word to Jesus of their brother's illness. When their brother got sick, they went straight to Jesus with their situation. A heart that has learned to recognize

27

and respond to an encounter with God has learned to seek Him first.

Notice the significance of the fact that Mary and Martha did not exhaust myriad other options before they finally decided to call on Him. He was their first and only option for help. When placed in a situation of fear and helplessness, their default position was that of calling out to God. They knew He was the only One who could truly answer them, so they didn't waste time looking for alternatives. Why would they waste time telling their problems to people who, at best, would be sympathetic to their circumstances but unable to do anything about them? They decided time was of the essence; they went straight to the only true Source of help: Jesus.

What is your Lazarus today? What situation in your life seems sick even unto death? Is it your marriage that is hanging on by a thread? Or maybe your children or other family members are spiritually sick and in need of a touch from Jesus? Whatever your situation may be, let me ask you, "Who is your source of help?"

The reason most of us don't go to God first with our problems is that we really don't expect Him to come through for us.

Often when we are in the midst of hard circumstances, we exhaust every option imaginable before we go to the One who not only hears and sympathizes with our plea but can also do something about it. Mary and Martha went to Jesus with their problem because they *expected* Him to come through for them. An expectant heart is one that calls out to the Lord first in times of need. It shows complete reliance on God. Expectancy is at the beginning of an encounter with God. I am convinced that the reason most of us don't go to God first with our problems is that we really don't expect Him to come through for us. We don't fully believe that He will show up and act on our behalf.

When situations arise in our lives that leave us fearful and bewildered, we often find that instead of going to the Lord we revert to some natural tendency or a specific habit to soothe us. A businessman might become introspective and unconsciously isolate himself from his family, or a woman in turmoil may immediately call a friend to share her thoughts. Often the sound of thunder during a rainstorm will make spouses huddle together in bed or a child run to his parents' bed in the middle of the night. In situations that stir our fears, each of us reverts to different habitual reactions. This is what Satan wants. He wants us to fill our place of need with every conceivable comfort except the Lord. In these comfortable places, we find some sense of security.

Unfortunately, we don't even think twice before we head to our default positions. Before we are aware of what we are doing, we have picked up the phone, snuggled next to our spouse in bed, or eaten that whole carton of ice cream! We need to learn to seek Jesus first. This must become our default position. I have decided that when I have a need in my life, I don't want to waste time. I want to see some results! That means I need to go to Jesus—better now than later, for time is too short.

Making Time

Not only must we seek Jesus, but we must also be deliberate in our approach. I am often amazed at how rushed and hurried the congregation seems when they come into Sunday morning service. I have done it myself. We come to church so tired from our week at work and worn thin from struggling with our families that morning. With sweat on our brows, it seems all we can do is collapse in the pew and await the sermon. We dread any part of the service that requires our participation because we just want to sit and soak. We have not taken the time to quiet our hearts or spirits. We are not prepared for the worship of a great Lord. We are just glad to be able to sit down. How dare we rush in to

29

worship the King of kings and Lord of lords in this manner! He deserves better than that, doesn't He?

I recall my mother asking me on several occasions when I came to worship half-prepared, "Priscilla, would that be your attitude if you were going to visit the president of the United States? If that is not how you would treat the president, then that is certainly not how you should treat the Lord." This principle applies not only at church but in our private worship as well. Is your quiet time something you fit in at the tail end of the day, if you are not too sleepy? Is it something you do in your car on your way to work, one eye on the road while the other is on a verse or two for the day? Or maybe you justify your lack of personal study by listening to your favorite radio pastors throughout your work-day. Their ministry is pertinent and extremely beneficial to the body of Christ, but Jesus wants personal time alone with you. I enjoy writing books and speaking, but I would never want this book or any other to take the place of your own personal study. You might incorporate read-ing materials into your special time with Him, but it should never replace your firsthand experience in the Word of God.

The Holy Spirit's job is to reveal very specific things to you through the Word that will "guide you into all truth" (John 16:13). Personal Bible study gives the Spirit a chance to work God's truth inside you. Do not allow the ministry of others to serve as your crutch. It's time for you to stop depending on "hand-me-down truth"—listening to and depending on what He has revealed to someone else. You have a spiri-tual right to receive firsthand revelation straight from the Lord. In order to make this happen, you and I have to prepare. You are going to have to schedule time with the Lord. Time to be still and quiet and clear your thoughts from the day. Time to make your way slowly and deliberately into the presence of the Lord, affording Him your full attention.

About four mornings a week, I arise at 5:30 A.M. to meet some friends for a morning run. I get up out of my warm, comfortable bed and brace myself for the cold, uninviting winds outside. I deliberately and cautiously set my alarm clock so that I wake up on time to exercise my body before the sun even rises. I do all of this work because I like the benefits of exercise. I like these benefits enough to make sure that exercise is a part of my day. In fact, it is so important to my friends and me that we don't schedule it at the end of the day; rather, we make it the first item on our list of things to do. We know that if we wait for the afternoon, we may be too tired or consumed with other things to remain committed.

You and I always make time for what is important to us.

You and I always make time for what is important to us, and we let other things slide. If you make time to spend with your significant other, make time for a meeting with your boss, make time to read your favorite novel or read to your kids before bed, then you have time to spend with Jesus. You just have to decide what is more important.

Turning Our Eyes upon Jesus

If we are really serious about our relationship with Jesus and His work in our lives, we must give Him our full attention, as Mary and Martha did. This lifts the veil from our eyes so that we can behold the encounters that we have with Him every day. Hundreds of years before Jesus even walked the earth, King Jehoshaphat had the right idea. When he was king over Israel, he found himself in a precarious position that caused him great anxiety. He was surrounded on all sides by an army that wanted to destroy the entire Jewish nation. As militarily strong as Israel had been in the past, he was still conscious of his inability to fight this war alone. He knew that unless Israel received some supernatural help, it was all over.

When Jehoshaphat heard the news of the impending danger, he did not withdraw from the masses, call a friend, or find refuge by snuggling up to his spouse for comfort. His default position was on his knees. "Alarmed, Jehoshaphat resolved to inquire of the LORD" (2 Chronicles 20:3). Just as Mary and Martha did centuries later, his natural tendency was to turn his attention to God. Here was the greatest man in Israel, the king, with anything and everything at his disposal, yet the Lord was the first and only thing that captured his attention in a time of fear. He sought the Lord because he knew God was the only one who could rectify his situation. He had incorporated his communication with God into the fabric of his life so that it was immediately on his mind when he became afraid. Years of complete reliance on God had formed this habit. It wasn't a spur-of-the-moment decision. He had formed the habit of turning his attention to God early, so it was a natural and normal tendency for him during a crisis.

What a lesson we can learn from this man who chose God over all else! We should always go to the Lord in prayer to show our complete reliance on Him. We should go to Him first, not after all of our other resources have been tried and have failed. We must be desperate for God and seek Him earnestly. King Jehoshaphat and Mary and Martha resorted to a default position on their knees, calling out to the Master for help.

Desperate for God

Jehoshaphat was so serious about his desire to see the Lord supernaturally come through for him and the people of Israel that he even went a step further. Second Chronicles 20:3–4 says, "He proclaimed a fast for all Judah. The people of Judah came together to seek help from the LORD."

Fear draws us to the point of total desperation. We have to be so desperate for the Lord to work in our lives that we not only turn our attention toward Him, but we also do whatever is necessary to make sure that He turns His attention toward us! To fast is to deny the needs of the flesh for a greater need of the spirit. It shows the Lord that you are serious about your request for His help and that you are willing to give up something you desire to ensure God's hand in your situation. It's time for us to be hungry for God. Blessed are those who hunger and thirst for righteousness, for they will be filled (Matthew 5:6).

It's time for us to be hungry for God.

Traditionally, Christians give up food, but you can also give up television, movies, certain books, or even chocolate for a season.

The point is to give up something that you long for to show the Lord that you do not take His involvement in your situation for granted.

The Lord declares that when you and I proclaim a fast in our lives, "'Then your light will break forth like the dawn, and your healing will quickly appear; then your righteousness will go before you, and the glory of the LORD will be your rear guard. Then you will call, and the LORD will answer; you will cry for help, and he will say: Here am I'" (Isaiah 58:8–9). The Lord takes it seriously when His children fast. If you want to encounter God like never before, then show the Lord that He is indeed more important than another priority in your life.

My husband, Jerry, recently made a decision that humbled me. He said he felt the Lord calling him to fast about a few things, such as our family, clear direction in the future, and upcoming career decisions. Most important, he wanted the Lord to galvanize a healthy fear and love for Him in his life. I told my husband that he should do it, thinking he meant a normal fast of food for three days. However, what my husband told me next startled me. He said that he felt the Lord calling him to fast not only food but also to fast his "life." He felt the Lord calling him to get away from his job, the comfort of his home, telephone, television, computer, food, and me too! He sensed that God wanted him to go to an undisclosed location where there were no comforts, no distractions, and no food for three days just to spend some time alone with the Lord and to hear His voice.

I must admit that I tried to make sure he had really heard the Lord on this! I thought that surely twenty-four hours would be sufficient. Three days seemed a little excessive. For a people-oriented person like me, that seemed like an impossible task. No connection with the outside world for three whole days?! However, Jerry was steadfast in his decision, and for three days he spent time alone with the Lord.

Jerry wanted to capture the Lord's attention, and the depth of his desire to hear from Him meant taking extreme measures. He was desperate! It was tough, but he was willing to give up all of those things because of his greater desire to hear from God. I am still humbled by this man who so loves the Lord that he was willing to do whatever it took to capture His attention. Jerry didn't want to waste time talking to anyone about his problems; he just wanted to hear from his Master. And hear from Him he did.

Satan knows that if you ever see the Lord in His fullness you will be changed and useless for him.

Upon my husband's arrival at the hotel where he chose to stay for those three days, he was surprised to hear a knock on the door. He was shocked since he hadn't told anyone where he would be. He opened the door to find that the hotel had sent up a complimentary basket of fruit. They left that tempting and succulent basket outside the room of a man on a three-day fast! It was apparent to my husband that the devil was doing his best to keep him from fasting and thus receiving the fullness of what the Lord had to offer him. Please be aware that Satan also knows the power of prayer and fasting, and he will do anything to detour you from doing so. He doesn't want you to be prepared to encounter the presence of God in your life. Satan knows that if you ever see the Lord in His fullness you will be changed and useless for him.

When I am afraid in life's battles, I desire that my unconscious habit will be to call out to the Lord and to allow all else to fall by the wayside as I look expectantly to God for answers. Whenever we have Lazarus situations, we must be confident that the Lord will want to do something in our lives to demonstrate His power. We must live expectantly. Life becomes so exciting when we realize we are on the cusp of an experience with God.

CHAPTER TWO

Be open, healed

The
CHANGE

May I be open, alert to change & serve You always

On his arrival, Jesus found that Lazarus had already been in the tomb for four days. Bethany was less than two miles from Jerusalem, and many Jews had come to Martha and Mary to comfort them in the loss of their brother. When Martha heard that Jesus was coming, she went out to meet him, but Mary stayed at home.

"Lord," Martha said to Jesus, "if you had been here, my brother would not have died. But I know that even now God will give you whatever you ask."

John 11:17–22

COULD IT BE YOU ARE READY to make the change? Have you determined in your heart to step out and away from the crowd around you, to be different and live a life of unbridled devotion to God? A caterpillar may spend as long as several days spinning silk and making its cocoon. Inside the warm darkness over the next one to several weeks, the transformation takes place. In the same way He works in nature to produce change, God may want to concentrate on a certain area of our lives where He desires a change. It may be our finances, our dating relationships, or our work. When we decide to turn our attention to Him and get serious about focusing on Him in an area of life, we may enter a cocoonlike experience to signal that God is at work.

For example, if you are single, He may put your dating relationships on hold for a period of time. You may not meet anyone, and your social life may dwindle compared to the world's standards. You might wonder, *What's going on here? Where did all the Prince Charmings go?* Sometimes God has to put another area of your life, such as your finances, in a cocoon in order for Him to alter the way you use your material resources. He does not bring that promotion or raise your way just yet. He does not allow you to buy that home you really want just yet. Everything is on hold until you encounter Him and allow Him to transform your perspective on money.

When you are in the middle of a cocoon experience, you may feel abandoned. Things may seem to be at their worst—dark, isolated, and lonely. As a new mom, I have discovered how it feels to be at home with a small baby all day long. That can make you feel isolated, for sure. All around you are little fingers, little toes, little words, and little toys. Everything is little! It can drive you crazy . . . or you can realize that God is up to something in your life and that all of your experiences are leading to the fulfillment of His will for you.

Picture the caterpillar in its cocoon, hanging there from a tree limb. It doesn't know what's happening to it; it doesn't know what's going on. It's just doing what God created it to do and waiting to see what happens next. Like the caterpillar, you may begin to feel isolated during your own cocoon experience, perhaps even uneasy as you wait alone in the darkness. Others all around you may be getting engaged to be married. Others may be climbing up the corporate ladder and moving up in the world financially. We wonder if God sees what is happening. Has He forgotten about us in the cocoon? When will we

"What the caterpillar calls the end of the world, the Master calls a butterfly."

—Richard Bach

come forth? During that cocoon experience, we can only say with confidence that God is at work in our lives, and we are waiting to see what happens next.

The Certainty of His Love

God began to work in Mary and Martha's situation long before they recognized His hand. John 11:5–6 says, "Jesus loved Martha and her sister and Lazarus. Yet when he heard that Lazarus was sick, he stayed where he was two more days." Those two phrases seem contradictory, don't they? It seems that if Jesus really loved them as much as He claimed, He would have immediately rushed to their side and healed their brother instead of purposely delaying. When He finally did show up, Lazarus was already dead.

What great despair Mary and Martha must have felt! They were sad because of the loss of their brother, and they were disappointed that their friend Jesus had seemingly let them down. How could He have done that? Martha spoke plainly when she said to Jesus upon His arrival, "Lord, if you had been here, my brother would not have died" (John 11:21). Martha was displeased that He had chosen to delay His arrival instead of coming to them immediately. In their grief, Mary and Martha were distracted from the deep truth tucked away in verse 5: "Jesus loved Martha and her sister and Lazarus."

There are three words that will give you hope in time of despair and will carry you through your cocoon experience. Take these three words with you at all times and in all situations. These three words can save your life: *Jesus loves me.* When you remain keenly aware of the fact that Jesus loves you, then you know He is on your side. When you know

He is on your side, you can then find peace in the midst of life's storms. His boundless love must serve as the foundation for our lives, so that even when times get bad, we can still rest in His declaration.

When Jesus loves you, then you can rest assured that all will be well with you. If the same Jesus who keeps the stars hanging in the sky and causes the earth to continue to spin on its axis . . . if that same Jesus, who keeps the planets in their orbit and makes sure that humans have enough air to continue to breathe day after day . . . if that same Jesus is in love with you, then what could you possibly have to fear? The Master of the universe is on your side. If He can handle all of that, then surely we can rest assured that He can handle our little situation as well!

Do you understand that when Jesus loves you, it doesn't matter how bleak your circumstances appear? It doesn't matter how dark life looks from the inside of the cocoon. He loves you so much that He gave His life for you. And the best part about His loving sacrifice is that He did it "while we were still sinners" (Romans 5:8). He didn't wait for us to clean up before He shed His blood for us. He did it while we were still a hopeless mess! He died for you when you had purposed in your heart to continue in a lifestyle of rebellion against Him, when you had chosen to disregard Him and turn away from His offer of salvation. When you were at your lowest point of disobedience and sin, He chose the nails! That is how much He loves us!

The Lord's declaration of love for us should set the tone of our lives.

Jesus declared His love for Mary, Martha, and Lazarus. He was crazy about them and had an everlasting and special affinity for these three. The Lord's declaration of love for us should set the tone of our lives. Are you inside a cocoon, undergoing changes all around that you just don't understand? Remind yourself on a regular basis that Jesus Christ, the King of all kings, is madly in love with you. Jesus has your best interests in mind. Remember that His declaration of love to you was written on a cross two thousand years ago, and it was signed with the ink of blood that flowed from His veins. That signature can never fade or be erased. Even when it seems like your situation is getting drastically worse, even when it seems that He is not showing up in a timely matter, remember that He loves you!

His love can supersede your sorrow.

His love can supersede your hurt.

His love can supersede your pain.

His love can supersede your impatience.

His love can supersede your frustration.

His love can change *you* in your circumstances!

Thank God that it doesn't matter what my past looks like, it doesn't matter what my present situation is, and it doesn't matter what my future will be . . . *He loves me.* I find hope in knowing this, and I thank God for His endless pursuit of me. "For I am convinced that neither death nor life, neither angels nor demons, neither the present nor the future, nor any powers, neither height nor depth, nor anything else in all creation, will be able to separate us from the love of God that is in Christ Jesus our Lord" (Romans 8:38–39).

The Waiting Process

Jesus was going to show up on the scene, all right. He was going to raise Mary and Martha's brother, Lazarus, from the dead. His love was so great for these three that He wanted to show them the most awesome miracle possible . . . so He made them wait. Sometimes, when it seems that the Lord is taking too long to show up in our Lazarus circumstances, it may be His love and grace providing an unexpected opportunity for the most incredible miracle of our lives. If you find yourself in a cocoon right now, you can be sure God is at work.

I believe Jesus' decision to make Mary and Martha wait for Him was a direct outpouring of His love for them. He didn't answer them on their timetable; rather, He allowed them to wait for something better. They knew that He could heal a sick man. They had already seen Him do that time and time again. Jesus wanted to show them that He was capable of more. He had power over death! They had never before seen this miracle.

In the same way that the caterpillar cannot settle into its life as a commonplace caterpillar, so too we cannot settle into life as usual if we follow God's plans for our lives. No, God's plans for both the caterpillar and for us are much bigger than that! Just as the caterpillar, when it enters the cocoon, has no idea that an incredible miracle lies ahead, so too we have no idea what God is up to in our lives while we are waiting for the miracle He wants to do.

He wants to do "immeasurably more than all we ask or imagine, according to his power that is at work within us" (Ephesians 3:20). God may cause you to wait, allowing the situation to get so bad that when He does show up, His miracle is even more astounding than if He had come earlier. So don't complain about the waiting process. Just get ready for a miracle beyond your wildest imagination! He wants to do something that you have never seen before.

If you are in the cocoon of waiting right now in some area of your life, please remember that Jesus is *allowing* you to wait so that His greater purposes may be served. He has not forgotten about you, nor has He become more consumed with other things. He is still in control. You must believe that and rest firmly in His promises in Scripture that declare this truth. Don't focus on the fact that you are waiting. Rather, focus your attention on the *reason* you are waiting. Changing your perspective can change everything!

Sandy was a secretary at our church for many years. She was actively involved in many areas and served her church family and nuclear family very faithfully. After over thirty years of marriage, her husband chose to leave his family for a blatantly rebellious lifestyle. In doing so, he chose to leave the church, his friends, and his relationship with Christ. However, Sandy resolved to keep praying for the man whom she had known intimately for most of her life. Although distraught by these uncontrollable and hurtful circumstances, she chose to believe Jesus loved her. He was indeed in control and had her best interests in mind.

Despite the heartache and pain, she chose to pray and wait on the Lord to revive her ex-husband and restore his spiritual life. Humbly, I must confess that I might not have been as faithful as Sandy to keep praying for my husband. I am amazed at her patience and sheer tenacity to keep her eyes and attention focused on the Lord during this four-year ordeal.

At the end of the fourth year, I remember sitting in church one Sunday, looking behind me at a man who sat quietly by himself. He looked very familiar, but I wasn't certain who he was. I smiled and turned back around in my seat as I tried to place his face. Suddenly it hit me! The man was Sandy's ex-husband. That bright Sunday afternoon the pastor called him up to receive the right hand of fellowship from our church as he was restored back into the family of God. What an exciting time as he renewed his commitment to the Lord and repented from his lifestyle of sin. We celebrated the restoration of this man into the body of Christ. Yet what happened next stirred our spirits to the core.

Sandy walked down the aisle in a plain, champagne-colored suit, graciously ascended the stairs, and met the pastor and her repentant ex-husband at the altar. Her children and grandchildren also came forward and stood beside both of them as the pastor remarried them!

Through tears and shouts of joy, the entire congregation spontaneously rose to our feet as we witnessed a resurrection of life and love. God allowed us to see the miracle of resurrection right before our very eyes! That day we knew 2 Corinthians 1:9 is indeed true: "But this happened that we might not rely on ourselves but on God, who raises the dead." I am certain that this man was resurrected because Sandy sought Jesus first. She turned her attention to the Lord, showed Him she was serious, and expected Him to come through. Yes, she had to wait years for restoration, but God had a miracle in store, not only for her benefit but also to edify all of us who watched that day and the many others who have heard of this miracle since then. We witnessed the power of God to change any circumstance and any situation, regardless of its severity. And God did it only in His time and only for the sake of His glory.

> "There is nothing in a caterpillar that tells you it's going to be a butterfly."
>
> —Anonymous

Can you imagine waiting that long for your husband to return? I am sure Sandy experienced a range of emotions: loneliness, discouragement, frustration, and anger while in her cocoon. Are these the emotions that you feel today? Are you mad that you are in a bleak situation? It is understandable to feel those emotions, but we must not let those emotions keep us from doing the right thing. Feelings must never be allowed to dictate our actions. Unswerving faith in God's Word alone must determine our actions.

When you trust and wait on the Lord, He will not only restore to you what was once lost; in His infinite grace and mercy, He will also give you much more than what you could have ever expected. In my last correspondence with Sandy, she confessed she could never have imagined during those years of trouble what rich blessings God had in store

> *"For my thoughts*
>
> *are not your*
>
> *thoughts, neither*
>
> *are your ways my*
>
> *ways,' declares*
>
> *the Lord"*
>
> *(Isaiah 55:8).*

for her and her husband. Sandy has seen tenfold the mercies of God in her life, a hint of what heaven holds for us. You and I can experience His abundant mercy, too!

In the waiting process it becomes easy to believe that God may not do what you want Him to do. However, as mere humans, we cannot determine what circumstances will unfold in our lives or how God will use them. I wish I could tell you that whatever you are going through will work out in the way that you would like it to, but I can't. Sometimes the way we want it to work out is not the way that God wants it to work out. We must trust that He is good, He loves us, and He knows what is best for us.

Jesus said to her, "Your brother will rise again."
John 11:23

What a powerful statement! Jesus' words are simple and to the point and show that God is indeed able to simply say the word and bring about life. God is *able*. Get that into your spirit. God is able to do what you are asking Him to do. Even if He chooses not to act, there is great peace and hope for us in knowing that He can!

Your friends can't.

Your therapist can't.

Your mother can't.

Your father can't.

Your spouse can't.

Your pastor can't.

But God can!

God is able. How He answers your need is only a question of His sovereignty, not His ability. If God chooses a different way to respond to your prayer than what you had wished, resolve to serve Him anyway. Martha had the faith to believe that Jesus could raise her brother from the dead.

The Refiner's Fire

Can you imagine how much more faith Mary and Martha had after this experience? After they witnessed Jesus' raising their brother from the dead, what could possibly happen to shake their faith in the future? After this situation their faith had deepened, and their knowledge of their Lord had been made concrete. Their suffering was God-allowed and God-ordained for the purpose of manifesting His greater glory in their lives. Jesus did not allow them to suffer needlessly. He allowed suffering to take place in order to provide the backdrop that He needed to do something really incredible. Because of His love, He also allowed the suffering to produce change in each individual. The more difficult your Lazarus circumstances may become, the more you need to thank God for His love. He has something in His bag of blessings just for you, and He is preparing you to receive it! James 1:2–4 reminds us that we can be joyful when the hard times come, because it is in persevering that we are made "mature and complete, not lacking anything."

"He will sit as a refiner and purifier of silver" (Malachi 3:3).

There is another great lesson to learn from the reason Jesus allowed them to wait for two days before His arrival. He would not have allowed them to go through more than He knew they could handle. A silversmith's job is long and tedious. He must pay close attention to detail, to even the smallest facets, in order for the masterpiece to be acceptable at its completion. Refinement is the art of ridding an object of impurities. The silversmith desires to bring forth the metal in its truest, flawless form. So when the silversmith places the object in the fire, he must stay nearby and watch diligently to see exactly how much heat the metal can endure. At just the right moment, he must remove the object from the fire before his precious metal is damaged.

Our divine Silversmith often places us in the fire—a place that seems too much for us to handle. The intense heat of our marriage, children, career, finances, or relationships might seem to be scorching the very life out of us, but we must take courage in knowing that He is sitting nearby. He is paying close attention to the heat He has *allowed* to engulf us. "No temptation has seized you except what is common to man. And God is faithful; he will not let you be tempted beyond what you can bear. But when you are tempted, he will also provide a way out so that you can stand up under it" (1 Corinthians 10:13).

The silversmith continues to heat the metal, burning away the impurities, until a precise moment when he knows his work is complete. There is only one way that he knows for certain that the work is complete: he can see his reflection clearly in it.

God's interest is always to make us look more and more like His Son. He desires to use all of our circumstances, good and bad, in such a way that we are refined into people who reflect Christ clearly. No matter what your circumstances look like, you must always remember there is something bigger going on than what you can see today. This means you and I have to humble ourselves in the midst of the fire so that the divine Silversmith can get busy and begin His work.

Paul said in Philippians 2:5–8, "Your attitude should be the same as that of Christ Jesus: Who, being in very nature God, did not consider equality with God something to be grasped, but made himself nothing, taking the very nature of a servant, being made in human likeness. And being found in appearance as a man, he humbled himself and became obedient to death—even death on a cross!" Although Jesus did not relish the thought of dying on a cross, He allowed the Silversmith to do His work. And so Jesus the Christ, the very Son of God, who held perfection and power in His hands, still subjected Himself in humility to the refining process (Hebrews 12:2). This is where He found true freedom and joy—in His Father's will.

The Master Refiner will burn away our impurities so that when He peers into us, He sees a reflection of His Son.

The same is true for us. No matter how difficult the "cross" ahead looks, the will of God is the only place where you and I will find true peace. This is where the transformation takes place. The Master Refiner will burn away our impurities so that we can be perfect and complete, lacking in nothing, so that when the great Silversmith peers into us, He sees a reflection of His Son.

Encountering Jesus

When he had said this, Jesus called in a loud voice, "Lazarus, come out!" The dead man came out, his hands and feet wrapped with strips of linen, and a cloth around his face.

Jesus said to them, "Take off the grave clothes and let him go."

John 11:43–44

Even though Mary and Martha were likely religious Jews, since they lived just outside Jerusalem in Bethany, they realized through this

Religious laws had nothing to do with what took place that day. It was Jesus.

one, life-changing encounter that Jesus could do what religion could never do. They and the rest of the crowd standing outside of Lazarus's tomb that day had never seen anything like this. Jesus raised Lazarus from the dead! Religion does not have the ability to change us; Jesus alone has unlimited resources to make a sweeping transformation of our lives with a single encounter. Religion is all about legalism, confined by strict rules and regulations; a relationship with Jesus stems from a deeply rooted love. You can be sure that family and that town were never the same after that day. They learned that their religious laws had nothing to do with what took place that day. It was Jesus.

We must make certain that we are not relying on the culture or tradition of religion to substitute for having a relationship with the One of whom our religion speaks. It is not good enough to know the Bible, to be dedicated in your church attendance, or to serve in a ministry at church. While those things are nice, they do not equal knowing Him. Jesus once told the Pharisees, "You diligently study the Scriptures because you think that by them you possess eternal life. These are the Scriptures that testify about me, yet you refuse to come to me to have life" (John 5:39–40).

It is not enough to know the information of the Bible. We must know its Author and be in love with Him. Therein is the difference between religion and relationship.

When God shows up, people change! It is impossible for people to be the same after they come in contact with a holy, loving God and see His hand in their lives. Even the ungodly feel rattled when the presence of God is near.

Armies tremble.

Nations fall.

Victories are won.

The lame walk.

The blind see.

The deaf hear.

The unsaved repent.

The dead are resurrected.

When God comes near, there is an obvious trail that tells of His visit. When He performs a Lazarus miracle in our lives, we should be changed and drastically different. What has He done for you? Remember when He . . .

resurrected your hope

resurrected your marriage

resurrected your finances

resurrected your children's spiritual lives

resurrected your career

resurrected your health

resurrected your heart for Him.

An encounter with God is life-altering. When He raises your Lazarus situation and overwhelms you with His boundless love and power, there should be a radical difference in your lifestyle and attitude of worship. You should . . .

work differently

play differently

react differently

measure success differently

eat differently

love differently

parent differently

spend money differently

serve differently.

Every aspect of your life should be different from the lives of those who do not know Him. Mary, Martha, and Lazarus were radically changed by their encounter with Jesus. We should be, too.

changed attitude

A New Way to
SERVE

May You open my mind, heart + soul to change my attitude + serve you

"[God makes] His ministers a flame of fire." Am I ignitable? God
deliver me from the dread asbestos of "other things." Saturate me
with the oil of the Spirit that I may be aflame. But flame is transient,
often short-lived. Canst thou bear this my soul—short life? In me
there dwells the spirit of the Great Short-Lived, whose zeal for God's
house consumed Him.

—Jim Elliot (1927–1956), missionary martyr to the Auca Indians, from
his college diary

Consider any suffering a learning opportunity
Be grateful.

JIM ELLIOT, missionary and lover of God, wrote these words about
giving up everything for God when he was a student at Wheaton
College. Don't read his statement too quickly. In fact, go back and read
it one more time. It is incredible! This man, long before his life was
taken, seemed to have spiritual insight into what his life might hold. He
clearly said that he wants to be set on fire to serve Christ and recognized
that if he is distracted by "other things," this will never happen.

He asked the Lord to deliver him from the death trap, the suffocation, the mind-numbing "dread asbestos" of things that might quell the flame to serve the Lord wholeheartedly. You see, our spiritual enemy, Satan, wants us to be so busy working *for* the Lord that we miss out on what matters most: our relationship *with* the Lord. The temptation of wrong priorities is high on the devil's list. In fact, I am certain this is Satan's biggest attack on those who desire to live the victorious Christian life. He wants us to think that the life we can conjure up for ourselves will both fulfill us and be satisfactory to God.

However, Jim Elliot found the secret of a life that is pleasing to God. He discovered that being singularly focused on God allowed him to experience the fullness of God while here on earth. He knew at an early age what most of us take a lifetime to discover. We find freedom in life only when we seek the Lord with all of our might, no matter what it costs us . . . even if the price we have to pay is our very life. Jim recognized that flames often go out very shortly after they ignite. However, knowing that he might have to risk everything to remain aflame for Christ, he asked the Holy One to saturate him with the oil of the Spirit of God so that, even if his life were cut short, his tombstone might read, "The spirit of the Great Short-Lived, whose zeal for God's house consumed Him." There is no denying that this man had certainly encountered God, and his life was forever changed.

> *We find freedom in life only when we seek the Lord with all of our might, no matter what it costs us.*

An encounter with God should change your priorities. What has the Lord called you to do in your life? What are the instructions that He has given you for serving Him? Drop everything else immediately and be obedient. Get rid of anything that is keeping you from serving God wholeheartedly. For each person it will be different. Is the money you

[handwritten margin note: spontanecity / my resentment + / to speak w/o / thinking makes me ugly + / hurtful]

are making in your great job keeping you from starting that ministry God has called you to do? Then the money has to go . . . today! Is fear keeping you from letting go of a destructive relationship? Then fear has to go . . . today! Is guilt from your past keeping you from moving full speed ahead into your blessed future? Then guilt has to go . . . today!

An encounter with God should cause us to put aside any and every thing that keeps us from putting a high priority on serving the Lord in the way He has planned for us. We need to ask the Lord to make clear what His priorities are and then keep our eyes focused on His answer. *[handwritten margin note: 55 + / Catholic / Church]* Anything that is a priority to you but is not also a priority to God will not satisfy you in the end. You may keep fruitlessly striving after those things, and they may satisfy you . . . but only for a little while.

The only thing that can satisfy your thirst for abundant life is serving Him and receiving what He has for you. This is why many people accumulate masses of wealth yet still feel unfulfilled and unsatisfied. Our culture produces people whose insatiable desire for worldly success is never satisfied nor met. Americans are the richest people in the world, yet they are also the most depressed and emotionally scarred. Why? Because we are striving after things that cannot satisfy the way only the things of God can!

Before Martha Changed

The first time we meet Martha in Luke 10, she invites Jesus to her humble home in Bethany for a dinner with her sister, Mary, and her brother, Lazarus. However, this dinner invitation soon eclipsed what should have been her first priority—being with Jesus.

> As Jesus and his disciples were on their way, he came to a village
> where a woman named Martha opened her home to him. She had
> a sister called Mary, who sat at the Lord's feet listening to what he
> said. But Martha was distracted by all the preparations that had to

be made. She came to him and asked, "Lord, don't you care that my sister has left me to do the work by myself? Tell her to help me!"

"Martha, Martha," the Lord answered, "you are worried and upset about many things, but only one thing is needed. Mary has chosen what is better, and it will not be taken away from her."

Luke 10:38–42

If we decide to focus on Jesus, what will we let go or how can we make this a priority?

Martha knew the "other things" Jim Elliot referenced all too well. There were dishes to be done. Pots to stir. Potatoes to peel. Plates to fill. Mouths to feed. We must realize that a good portion of those things we feel really need to get done on our watches will have to go undone in order to focus on the most important things. It's easy to feel so wiped out serving your ministry at church or the local PTA that you have no quality energy and time left for your family—your first ministry. It's easy to become so overwhelmed preparing to teach a Sunday school lesson each week that we neglect our own daily quiet time with the Lord.

The Lord has begun to impress upon me the importance of this in my own life, and I have been challenged to shake off the excess from my life so that I too can just sit at His feet as Mary did. This has been a difficult thing for me. It has meant that I must sometimes go without meeting my girlfriends for lunch or shopping, or that I must go without my favorite television show. Some days my housework must go undone (yea!) so that I can spend time with Him and be prepared to minister to others. Thank God for my understanding husband!

What He may ask you to give up will be different from what He has required of me. Your responsibility is to simply respond to the conviction of the Holy Spirit in your life. What is He asking you to put aside for His sake?

Don't let your personal schedule and tasks override the real reason you were put on this earth—fellowship with the Father, found by living

Don't let your

personal schedule

and tasks override

the real reason

you were put on

this earth—

fellowship with

the Father.

in obedience to Him. There is nothing wrong with earthly things having their place; just make sure it's second place. God created Martha to be a servant, no doubt. I believe this was her spiritual gift. However, He wanted to make sure Martha's role as a servant didn't override her primary calling to be in relationship with Him.

After Martha Changed

> Here a dinner was given in Jesus' honor. Martha served. . . .
>
> John 12:2

The next time we encounter Martha is in John 12, after Jesus had raised her brother from the dead, and she is still serving. Still cooking. Still hustling and bustling. It seems that some things had changed and others had not. Martha, Mary, and perhaps other women got together and prepared supper for Jesus, but when Jesus arrived, Mary and the other women decided that their kitchen duty was over! Verse 2 indicates that Martha alone served. Poor Martha! She seems to get a hard time from everyone about her serving, but we have to consider that this was her spiritual gift and her ministry.

Maybe you need to let go of some things, follow Mary's example, and just come sit at Jesus' feet. I have news for you: If you let some things go on your schedule, the world will go on without you! While serving is not necessarily bad, Jesus just wished that Martha would do less serving at the moment. On His first visit, He even warned her that she was "worried and upset about many things" (Luke 10:41). Jesus made it clear to her that the better thing was to fellowship with Him rather than to take all of her time preparing for Him. He much prefers intimacy with those who love Him. Although I am sure that her intentions were right during Jesus' first visit to her home, she was taking too much time cooking a twelve-course meal when Jesus would have been fine with a casserole! He just wanted to spend time with her.

So when we see her here in Jesus' second visit, it seems as if Martha has not changed. It seems as if she is still busy serving just as she was before her encounter with Jesus. However, only Jesus could see her true motive for serving and working so diligently in the kitchen, and I believe that what He saw on this day was different from what He'd seen in the past. Jesus did not rebuke her here in John 12, so we can assume something had changed. Although her actions were the same, the attitude with which she served was completely different. Now her ministry of service was fervent, loving, and sincere. Her heart must have been in the right place because this time she was serving without a word of complaint.

Back in Luke 10 when the Lord rebuked Martha for her serving, He had done so because of her complaining. It wasn't her service that was wrong; it was her attitude. She had said, "Lord, don't you care that my sister has left me to do the work by myself? Tell her to help me!" She was serving the Lord all right, but she was doing so with a bad attitude. Have you ever met someone who serves with a bad attitude? Surely not *you*, right?

The Lord does not want our service unless we are going to do it unto Him. Do you complain about the ministry you serve in at the church? Do you complain about your role as wife? Do you complain about your role as mother? We need to be reminded that our service is not for those physical beings such as our boss or spouse. Our service should be done with a joyful attitude unto the Lord. He notices our efforts and appreciates our work, even when others do not. The Bible says in 1 Peter 4:8–9, "Above all, love each other deeply, because love covers over a multitude of sins. Offer hospitality to one another without grumbling."

Here's the secret to serving with the right attitude: take your eyes off the physical people you are serving, and place your eyes solely on the One whom you must ultimately serve. Before she knew better, Martha had allowed herself to become frustrated because she had taken her eyes off the true recipient of her service. Sometimes your husband will appreciate you, and sometimes he will not. Sometimes your children will thank you, but many times they will not. Sometimes the people in your life will applaud your efforts, and sometimes they won't. When you find that a spirit of complaining is overtaking you in what the Lord has called you to do, take a personal inventory. Whose praise are you attempting to receive? Who are you trying to impress with your labor? Could you have forgotten that all of your work is for the Most High God?

Feel free to continue to use your gifts and talents, just as Martha did, but do so only as long as you are capable of doing it to God's glory. What are you called to be? A wife? A mother? A CEO? An athlete? What are you called to do? If God has called you to be a mother, then teach your children for God's glory. If God has called you into the corporate world, then supervise your staff and manage your accounts to God's glory. Ask the Lord to make clear to you those things that are not pleasing to Him so that you can adjust accordingly and have more time for those things that are.

Only what is done for Christ will last.

Scripture makes clear that only what is done for Christ will last. Only those activities and pursuits that you perform with the mindset of gracious obedience to the Lord will stand before His throne. Everything else will have been a waste of your time.

I must admit that one of my greatest fears is to get to heaven, stand before the Lord, and find that what I spent my time doing while on earth was not what God intended for my life.

What a waste of time and energy for me to spend my life doing things that will be rubbish before His throne on the day when I see Him face-to-face. An encounter with God must change the way we spend our lives serving Him. I continually seek the Lord in this regard and give Him freedom to change my direction at any time. I don't want to spend my life doing what I think is good only to find out that it wasn't what He had in mind.

Serving Without a Word

John 12 shows us a new Martha whose actions were the same but whose attitude was different. We find not a word of complaint in John 12. In the same way, God is asking us to serve Him without any complaint. Your tongue is one of the most powerful instruments in your body. You can use it to build up or to tear down, to create or to destroy, to construct or deconstruct. How are you using your tongue? What good is cooking your family a meal for dinner if all they remember about dinner time is how much Mommy and Daddy argued about their busy day? What good is your work in the music ministry in your church if all that the alto section knows about you is how terrible your day was every time you come to rehearsal? What good is our "service" to God if that mouth of ours destroys its value? The Lord has spoken clearly to me on this issue in James 3:2–6.

What good is our "service" to God if that mouth of ours destroys its value?

We all stumble in many ways. If anyone is never at fault in what he says, he is a perfect man, able to keep his whole body in check.

When we put bits into the mouths of horses to make them obey us, we can turn the whole animal. Or take ships as an example. Although they are so large and are driven by strong winds, they are steered by a very small rudder wherever the pilot wants to go. Like-wise the tongue is a small part of the body, but it makes great boasts. Consider what a great forest is set on fire by a small spark. The tongue also is a fire, a world of evil among the parts of the body. It corrupts the whole person, sets the whole course of his life on fire, and is itself set on fire by hell.

I think the heart + soul controls our tongue

James tells us quite plainly that although the tongue is one of the smallest instruments in our intricately designed bodies, it can destroy us! James says that the tongue is like a small spark that creates a raging forest fire. Is there a raging fire in your marriage, ministry, home, or job? Is your tongue setting the flame? My tongue is capable of setting a flame that not only defiles my body and those around me, but it also burns down my entire life! Our lives from birth to death can be destroyed if we choose to use our tongues inappropriately! There is power in your mouth. It can either be a weapon of destruction or a tool of blessing and encouragement. Martha's example reminds us that we must let God transform us so that we choose our words wisely.

I have to be very conscious of this area in my own life. I am not a quiet person by any means. I have always been an assertive, high-energy individual who makes my opinion known just a little too often some-times. Most of the times that I got in trouble growing up had to do with something that I said!

Now that I am in the role of wife, Proverbs 21:9 has scolded me many times. "Better to live on a corner of the roof than share a house with a quarrelsome wife." I don't want to be that wife. Life and death are in the power of my tongue, so I must speak life into my home, family, and work. My mouth is the gatekeeper for life!

"The tongue that brings healing is a tree of life, but a deceitful tongue crushes the spirit" discuss *(Proverbs 15:4).*

I remember going through a hard time in my relationship with Jerry early in our marriage. One day as I was praying about it . . . well, actually, I was praying *for* my husband. I felt that I had been uniquely gifted and anointed to change him! It was during one of these prayer sessions for Jerry that the Holy Spirit clearly told me that the problem was not him; it was me! He told me that victory in the situation would come when I learned to control my tongue. God instructed me that no matter how much I wanted to comment on my husband's actions or correct him, I was to support and serve him without a word. I was only to build him up and not say anything to tear him down, in private or in public. I have watched this principle make an enormous difference in the fabric of our relationship.

When I find that I am becoming argumentative and my words or tone about my work or circumstances are not life-giving words, I ask myself two questions. First, *"Have I taken my eyes off of the Lord?"* I actually make myself sit down and determine my focus. Am I trying to please God, myself, or someone else in this particular situation? Second, *"Do I need to continue in this service, or is the Lord calling me to spend my time and energy elsewhere?"* Frustration could be a signal that you are to move on from this task to another that the Lord has for you. It does not always signify the need for a change, but it could. Ask yourself these same questions. Obviously, there are some positions of service that you cannot change, like your position as wife or mother. However, oftentimes the reason our attitudes are not right in those areas is because we are wasting too much time in other areas, areas that we should consider cutting out of our lives. Like Martha, we are so busy serving that we have forgotten what is better.

After Martha's transformation, Jesus had no reason to correct her for her attitude or her service. We don't find a rebuke from Jesus as we did when they had met for dinner before. If you are a Christian woman, you can be sure that when you are outside the will of God for your life, He will let you know. The quiet prompting of the Holy Spirit will allow you to be aware of the Lord's desire for you to change what you are doing. I am frequently reminded by the Holy Spirit that my tongue has power in my marriage and family. Are you and I choosing to speak either a blessing or curse over our children and spouse? Are we bringing healing to our families, ministries, and friends, or do we crush the spirit of everyone around us? Could we even be destroying our own lives by the words that we choose to speak? Take a personal inventory. We must carefully monitor the words that flow from us. An anonymous author once wrote that wisdom is divided into two parts: one—having a great deal to say; two—not saying it!

What power we have in our tongues to change things for the better or for the worse! Choose to serve the Lord wholeheartedly, without a word of complaint. An encounter with God should change the way we serve Him.

CHAPTER FOUR

Deeper Intimacy with

JESUS

Here a dinner was given in Jesus' honor . . . while Lazarus was among those reclining at the table with him.

John 12:2

when others leave you, Jesus is there always.

THE LAST TIME Jesus had seen Lazarus, his body had been wrapped in burial linens. In fact, he had been dead for several days, and the stench of death was most likely unbearable. Needless to say, he was in bad shape when he encountered Jesus. He needed a miracle! Then Jesus called Lazarus' name, and Lazarus stumbled out of his tomb. He had received the gift of physical life from Jesus. Now in John 12, he wanted to receive spiritual life and nourishment from Him as well. We find him "reclining at the table" with Jesus. Physical food is good, but even better is the opportunity to recline at the table with the Bread of life. Lazarus' priority was deeper intimacy with Jesus.

Scripture declares that we have all at one time been dead in sin with the stench of our past clinging to us, yet He still longs for our fellowship and intimacy. Fortunately, His desire for a deep relationship is not dependent upon us. No matter how bad our past is, He still desires to be with us. If you are saved, it is only because Jesus demanded that the stone be removed from the door of your heart. He called you out of your cold tomb of darkness and into His brilliant salvation. You are spiritually alive because, in His boundless love for you, He chose to overlook and overcome the stench of your history.

It doesn't matter what age you were saved—your past was horrid compared with His holiness. You cannot feel superior if you were saved at five years old and never went through a period of rebellion. Likewise, don't feel judged and inadequate if you did live a blatantly sinful life before you met the Savior. In each instance, your sin looked equally horrid to Him. Yet He called you by name and saved you from it. In fact, Scripture says that the more dreadful your past was, the more intimate He expects and desires your relationship with Him to be (Luke 7:47). The more He has saved us from, the more we should want to be with Him.

The more He has saved us from, the more we should want to be with Him.

He has "called you out of darkness into his wonderful light" (1 Peter 2:9). You and I were formerly dead in our transgressions and sins (Ephesians 2:1), yet He loved us and called our names so that we no longer suffer the consequences for our sin. He gave us true life! I don't know about you, but, like Lazarus, I want to get to know Him intimately, reclining at the table with this Man who saved my life.

Jerry and I love to visit Chicago, especially the Magnificent Mile on Michigan Avenue. This street is named appropriately for its incredible shopping and restaurants. I must admit that when I get a chance to hang out on this famous street in Chicago, I always have one eye open for Oprah Winfrey! I know that she lives in Chicago, so I figure that it is very possible that I might catch a glimpse of her someday. I would love to meet her, but if I ever did come face-to-face with her, I would probably be speechless. What in the world do you say to Oprah Winfrey? I would probably stammer and stutter just to say hello and ask for a simple autograph.

Here was Lazarus, sitting next to Jesus, the Celebrity of the universe! I can imagine that he was speechless in awe of the One who had restored his very life. Forget human celebrities. I know the Celebrity of the universe, who also happens to be the One who saved my life. I am enamored with Him and Him alone. Halle Berry, Oprah Winfrey, Bill Cosby, Julia Roberts, Denzel Washington—who are they? They haven't done anything of value for me or for you. If we get sweaty palms over the thought of being in their presence, then how much more amazed should we be at the prospect of being in the presence of our Savior, the King of kings and Lord of lords? There is only one Celebrity of the universe, and His name is Jesus. I can only imagine how Lazarus must have felt in the presence of God that day.

It seems that Lazarus knew the beauty of being close with Christ. He chose not to sit across the table from Jesus that day. Rather, I like to think that he selected a seat that was as close as he could possibly get. I wonder if he received some special insight at dinner that night that others did not hear because he was the one sitting just beside the Lord. I want to be the one sitting beside the Lord. I don't want to hear what the public is privy to hear. I want the inside track. This means that I must choose to snuggle up close. And what is even more staggering about this scene is that Jesus allowed Lazarus to recline with Him. Jesus did not move to the other side of the table. He stayed there with a man who had once been a dead, decaying body. Oprah might run from an overzealous, adoring fan. . . . Jesus will not. He wants to meet with us. When we snuggle up close to Jesus, He won't forsake us; He will snuggle up close to us in return.

AND WE ARE CHANGED

You and I have the same privilege of being with Jesus whenever we please. We can relax in His presence and celebrate His holiness whenever we feel like it. In fact, you and I have it a lot better than Lazarus did that day. He had to share the Messiah's attention with the others who had gathered around that table. When you and I want to meet with Him, we have Him all to ourselves. He is at your full disposal when you recline at the table with Him. When God does something amazing in your life, like raising you from spiritual and physical death, you should allow nothing to come in the way of spending one-on-one, personal time with Him. This is an integral part of your Christian life. This is when the King will meet personally with you.

Intimate Relationship

I recall one day in 1997 when I was having a very difficult emotional experience. After two years of dating a young Christian man with promises of marriage, he called off the relationship. I was devastated. I clearly remember driving down the road and crying rivers of tears. I was hurt so badly because I missed my friend and wanted our relationship to work. I will never forget that day, because I heard the Lord clearly speak to me in my grief. He said, "He doesn't want you, and you still want to spend time with him. Yet I want you desperately, but you don't want to spend time with Me!"

I was stunned by the clear message from the Lord, and I was humbled that His love was pursuing me and had found me in my car! I continued to cry, but now the tears were those of conviction over my neglect of the One who wanted my intimacy. In my hurt, in my deep despair, and even in my sin, the Lord wanted me to take my attention off my pain and place it on Him. I had been so consumed by the situation that I hadn't really taken enough time to recline at the table and spend time with the One who was in control of my circumstances. This was the Lord's plea to me, and it is His plea to you! He wants you. Why won't you spend time with Him?

If you are married, you may know what it is like to sleep in the bed next to your husband and not want to touch or talk. You mentally draw an imaginary line and dare him to cross it at any time during the night! How unfulfilling and disappointing those times in any marriage are. I don't like them. God constructed marriage to be a loving, personal, intimate relationship, yet it is possible to be married but have no intimacy. I don't just want to be legally bound by a certificate. I want to have fellowship and be closely bound in spirit to my sweet man!

This is what Jesus wants with us as well. He didn't put the "wedding ring" of the Cross on your finger and strike a covenant with you so that you and He could be mere acquaintances. He did it so that your lives could be intertwined in the most intimate way possible. Jesus desires that you two be the best of friends and share a relationship like no other. He did not die on the cross just to save you from destruction. He died so that you could have an intimate relationship with Him. I am convinced that Lazarus' decision to recline at the table teaches us a valuable lesson about the priority that the Lord places on the time that He spends with us. An encounter with God should change our level of intimacy with Him.

CHAPTER FIVE

More Passionate
WORSHIP

Here a dinner was given in Jesus' honor. Martha served, while Lazarus was among those reclining at the table with him. Then Mary took about a pint of pure nard, an expensive perfume; she poured it on Jesus' feet and wiped his feet with her hair. And the house was filled with the fragrance of the perfume.

John 12:2–3

THE THREE TIMES we encounter Mary in the four Gospels, she is at the feet of Jesus. There is just something about being at the feet of Jesus, isn't there? We must lay down all that we are and all that we hope to be and humble ourselves before Him. Mary knew that the only true way to worship was to humble herself at His feet. I pray that I become like Mary, needing nothing but Jesus to make me feel fulfilled. I want to be satisfied in His presence, at His feet. In church, I don't want to require a great sermon or incredible music from the choir. I want to be satisfied with the indescribable gift of worshipping Him and knowing

what do I want/need to be fulfilled

71

that He accepts my worship. If we knew how to simply enjoy and revel in the presence of God, we would no longer need so many programs to fill the time during our church services.

God often meets us in the places that are most uncomfortable for us.

Being at the feet of Jesus is about humility. The lowly place of worshipping at the feet of Jesus does not come naturally for any of us. In our culture we don't often stoop to anybody's feet for any reason. In fact, the world encourages us to make sure we have one up on everybody else. We want people to be at our feet, following our lead, and eating our dust. To lower ourselves to the feet of someone else is the ultimate act of humility. It is not a comfortable place for fallen humans who always desire to be in the place of most importance. However, God often meets us in the places that are most uncomfortable for us, and when He shows up, people change.

At His Feet

I can remember two or three times at the most when I had a spiritual experience so great that I will never forget it. I had one such experience at a small women's conference where I was one of the main speakers.

One of the hardest things that I have to do sometimes in my work is travel alone. My husband or a close friend normally travels with me to take care of the "business aspect" of the trip so I can concentrate on ministering the Word of God, but for some reason it hadn't worked out that way this time.

By the time I arrived, the conference had been going on for three days. I soon discovered that they had somehow forgotten to display and sell my books. All the books were still tucked away in boxes underneath a table. Frustrated, I continued past the table and into the back of the room where the ladies were seated . . . all sixty ladies. That would have been fine with me, but they had told me to expect five hundred women there. Traveling alone and trying to lug around a couple of big boxes of leftover books (I had shipped enough for five hundred women) in a crowded airport is tough! There was no one there to help me with my books, the event was much smaller than I had expected, and I was having a hard time. Even though the ladies were very warm and tender in their words, for some reason I still felt very uncomfortable in this situation. I finally asked the Lord a very direct question. "Lord, why am I here?" I know that the Lord has a reason for everything, but I wanted to know specifically why the Lord had chosen to place me here.

Now, you need to understand the perspective that I am coming from. When I am invited to speak, it is normally for an audience of two thousand women or more. This is not a prerequisite for me to come and speak; it just seems that is where I end up most of the time. I don't say this in any way to speak highly of myself but only to illustrate my point. The conferences that I usually speak at are wonderfully organized. They fly in professional singers and elaborately decorate the stage. The book tables are organized and staffed by volunteers. The microphones are all checked to make sure that the sound system is in perfect working order, and the instrumentalists rival any symphony orchestra. It is amazing how quickly one can get used to such comforts.

This conference was none of the above. The singers who came to the microphone were little old ladies who just loved God. The qualification for becoming a member of this praise team was not vocal ability, and it showed. They sang several praise songs—all off-pitch and off-beat. I was amazed. I hadn't been in a situation like this in so long that it threw me off guard.

However, for the last song in the medley, a little old black lady led us in "Hail Jesus, You're My King." When this kind, sweet, Spirit-filled woman came to the microphone and began to belt out the words to this song an enormous smile made its way onto my face. I couldn't help it. There is nothing like an older woman singing the praises of the Lord. She doesn't have to be on key, and she doesn't have to know all the correct words. You can just hear the power of the Lord in her music. Well, my friend, the Lord knew that this was all that I needed. My spirits were lifted, and I ended up speaking with passion and purpose. Little did I know that I had not come simply to speak to those women that day. We were all about to have an encounter with God.

After my presentation, as most of us prepared to leave, it happened. God showed up. It started softly with one woman unreservedly but quietly singing praises to God. Then the sound of worship grew exponentially as more women began to join in. With tears streaming down their faces, one by one, these ladies began to spontaneously sing praises to God. Just like the ripple effect of a rock thrown into a pond, so the Holy Spirit's presence began to fill that place. For one whole hour, these sixty women from this small church were praising the Lord with all their might. As the presence of God filled the room, we called out to Him, worshipped Him, and repented of our sin. The presence of God felt so tangible, so thick, that it overwhelmed us. Many of the women could no longer stand. They knelt before the Lord. Some lay prostrate before Him, and some took off their shoes to signify that they knew the ground on which they stood was holy. These women did not care about whether or not the microphones were balanced or whether the program would end on time. No one was looking at her watch in disgust because the hour was growing late. Why? God was there. He had taken center stage.

God was there. He had taken center stage.

I have been at many large, well-organized conferences where people leave whether or not the speaker is finished, because they have "better things to do." These women showed me that they too had "better things to do," and the best thing was to sit at His feet. To experience Him. To position themselves to receive from Him. No orchestra—just the sweetness of the Holy Spirit. No professional singers—just the Most High God. No pomp and circumstance—just some women serious about meeting with the Master.

This scene forced me outside of my comfort zone and drove me to the feet of Jesus. I fell to my knees in this room among women who were serious about experiencing Him, and in their midst I felt unworthy. I repented. "Lord, forgive me for being caught up in the small things that don't matter anyway and for not concentrating totally on You. Please allow me to know You as these women know You. I am asking that I see You as they do. Master, this is my request. I want to know You more." In His holy presence, I caught a glimpse of my depravity. When God shows up, you begin to realize how needy you truly are. Like Isaiah, who saw the Lord and said, "'Woe to me! . . . I am ruined! For I am a man of unclean lips, and I live among a people of unclean lips, and my eyes have seen the King, the LORD Almighty'" (Isaiah 6:5).

I felt as if I too had seen the King. I stayed there on the floor for quite some time. I felt the presence of God there with me, thick like a cloud, so thick that I couldn't move. I was embarrassed and ashamed that such trivial and insignificant things as book sales, the number of women at the conference, and whether or not I was traveling alone almost kept me from encountering the fullness of the Lord that day. I was humbled that God used me to speak to these women who, in my estimation, were a whole lot closer to Him than I was.

Then I knew why I was there. God wanted to show me that outside of my comfort zone was exactly where He needed me to be in order to do supernatural things in my life. He needed me to reposition myself at His feet so that I could receive from Him. He also made it clear to me that He would rather be with sixty women who were serious about sitting at His feet and worshipping Him than with three thousand who were concerned about some religious program.

Being at Jesus' feet suggests our desire to put all else aside for a time so that we are right where we need to be to receive blessings from the Lord. We must ask God to forgive us for not taking seriously the beauty of sitting still, uninterrupted, single-minded, focused, and humbly positioned at His feet. It is there that He challenges us and calls us into a closer relationship with Him.

A New Level of Worship

In John 12, Mary is still at Jesus' feet, yet her worship has deepened to another level as a result of her encounter with Jesus at her brother's resurrection. She was still overwhelmed at His awesomeness, just as we should be. However, this scene is a little bit different from the times we have previously seen her. Back in Luke 10, she was sitting at His feet listening to His teaching. This time, instead of just sitting at Jesus' feet, she poured out her affection and adoration on His feet.

Worship has nothing to do with receiving; it has everything to do with giving.

Mary retrieved the most expensive perfume that she owned and poured it out over the feet of Jesus (John 12:3–8). She could not contain her love for this man, her Lord, who loved her so dearly that He brought her brother back to her again. She was willing to "waste" (as some would say) her most expensive possession for the sake of His glory.

When you and I deeply, sincerely worship the Lord, it is a sacrifice. Worship has nothing to do with receiving; it has everything to do with giving. You cannot come to the Lord clinging to all of the things you hold dear and still *really* worship the Master. Your most expensive and prized possessions have to be emptied out before your worship will be pleasing to God. You must pour out pride and jealousy. You must pour out anger and lust. Fear and resentment must be poured out. Idolatry must be poured out. To worship the Lord in all sincerity, you must be willing to take anything you treasure that is holding you back from worship and release it at the feet of Jesus. Then God can give you what He wants for you.

You must also release those things that are precious to you. That relationship must be poured out before Him. That ministry must be poured out before Him. Those finances must be poured out before His throne. Those desires and longings of your heart must be poured out so that you empty your hands of everything in order to make room for what He has for you. This is necessary and nonnegotiable.

> *Worship always involves your sacrifice of the thing that is most valuable to you.*

Mary did not just pick up any bottle of perfume from her vanity table; her worship was deliberate. She went and purposefully found the one that she treasured the most, the most expensive thing that was worth a full year's wage, the one she was saving for a very special occasion. That was what she sacrificed to the Lord. Worship always involves your sacrifice of the thing that is most valuable to you. It can hurt to get rid of those things, but John 4:23 says, "True worshipers will worship the Father in spirit and truth, for they are the kind of worshipers the Father seeks." The Lord desires to see that we are willing to give up the things we cherish the most for His sake. The humbling process of "pouring out" these things is difficult and scary, but it is worth it. What the Lord has in store for you will be far better than what you were holding onto anyway.

I have seen this principle of pouring out at work in my own life. I mentioned in an earlier chapter that I had considered marriage in a previous relationship. For quite a while I had felt the Lord telling me to let go of that relationship in faith, because He knew what was best for me. But I didn't want to do that. I continued that relationship, even though doing so meant incredible emotional pain for me. At the end of that relationship, when I was at an all-time emotional low, I asked the Lord to forgive me for disobeying Him, and I surrendered that relationship to Him. I will never forget that day as a seminary student when I got down on my knees in my room and just gave up. I let go of the most expensive and precious thing I had. As I offered God a part of me, the emotional pain was overwhelming, and I wept uncontrollably.

However, in that little room that day, God showed up, and I encountered Him. He cupped my face in His hands and wiped away my tears. He began to mend my heart. Since I had let go of what I wanted, there was room for what He wanted. Three months later, I met Jerry . . . the man that I would indeed marry.

Meeting Jerry changed my life and restored me. As the broken pieces of my past began to fall away, Jerry loved and affirmed me. The most incredible thing about our love story is that Jerry and I had been going to the same church for six years but had never met. It was almost as if the Lord was waiting for me to pour out my most expensive treasure so that He could give me true treasure indeed! My life and marriage are a testimony to the principle of pouring out our own dreams and plans before Him!

Letting Down Your Hair

It was all Mary of Bethany could do to contain herself. She wanted to do all she could to show her Lord how His love enraptured her, so she took her worship even one step further. She was willing to embarrass herself. John 12:3 says that she "wiped his feet with her hair." In those days, when a woman let down her hair, she disgraced her entire family, particularly her husband. In fact, she could have been stoned to death for such an act. Yet Mary was undeterred from her worship of the Master. She didn't seem to care what anyone else thought about her. She was determined to make her love for Him known.

Are you willing to look ridiculous for the sake of Christ? Are you and I so changed by the miracles that He has performed in our lives that we are willing to pour out our pride and reputation just to please God? Are you willing to let down your hair? I can remember being in college and feeling embarrassed to be the only one in opposition to certain societal principles that were popular among the professors and other students. It was tough, and I was not always as bold as I should have been. We will all find ourselves in tight spots in our workplaces or in our schools, and we will be ridiculed for what we believe. But are you, like Mary, so moved by God's goodness in your life that you couldn't care less about facing embarrassment for His sake?

We have to be bold for the sake of the One who surely was embarrassed for us.

In Romans 1:16, Paul writes, "I am not ashamed of the gospel, because it is the power of God for the salvation of everyone who believes." We have to be bold for the sake of the One who surely was embarrassed for us. Mary was serious about her worship and her relationship with Jesus, and she didn't care what others thought about her bold, impassioned statement.

My father is a speaker for Promise Keepers, which is a convention for men that takes place all over the country. He told me the story of one particular conference at which he spoke. That day, a big storm was supposed to hit the area. This was not good news, because about seventy thousand men had gathered in an open-faced stadium for the conference. As the ministers stood on the platform, they could see the storm clouds gathering on one side of the stadium. It looked as if they were indeed in trouble. If it began to rain, they would have to call off the function, at least for a while, in order to protect the very valuable electronic equipment that would not function well in the rain. The ministers who were on the program that day decided to go backstage and pray about the inclement weather and ask the Lord to keep the rain from falling so that the program might continue.

Here my dad stood, in the midst of this incredible medley of great men of God and other faithful believers who were volunteering at the event. They began to pray. The preachers prayed these incredible prayers that were rich in theological prowess. They used deep, spiritual lingo. Dad said that everyone tried to pray these incredible prayers that would have impressed anybody. They all prayed comfortable prayers that would keep them in the clear just in case it did rain that day at the stadium. However, when they were finished, a little woman who was just a volunteer at the event decided to pray as well. She said, "In the name of Jesus of Nazareth, I command that this storm not fall on this stadium today. Amen!" All of the ministers opened one eye to peek over at this woman as she prayed. She was serious and bold. There was no time for pomp and circumstance, no time for deep theology, no time for prayers said to impress. She wanted to get some results! That day the men had their conference in a dry stadium. They all watched the rain start falling several miles south of the stadium, stop raining as the clouds passed over the stadium, and then begin to rain again just north of them. That is the power of God! That power is available to all of us when we get serious about seeing God, risk embarrassment, and stand up as bold members of His family!

Some people are willing to die for what they believe in. How much more should you and I be willing to, at most, be embarrassed for the sake of the truth! When we become serious about our worship,

*Pray that
I let go + allow
God to change
me*

pomp and circumstance are irrelevant; whether or not you have a theological degree doesn't matter; what church you go to or what denomination you claim takes a back seat. You become willing to do whatever it takes to make sure that the Lord knows that you are serious—even if it requires looking foolish to the world.

Worship Alters the Environment

Don't overlook the fact that the fragrance of Mary's worship lingered in the air for all to enjoy. Her worship made her known, as "the house was filled with the fragrance of the perfume" (John 12:3). Her love for the Savior affected the entire environment. If you want to change the environment in your home, office, or school, then begin to worship God sincerely. Stop praying that God will change everyone else, and start turning your full attention to Him. The fragrance of your praise will rouse the hearts of others. The aroma of worship is sweet to the Lord and sweet to the one who extends it. It so penetrates the most remote corners of the place where it resides that it cannot be ignored or go unrecognized.

Now that I have a home of my own, I try to create a certain atmosphere there. I have visited huge homes that were elaborately decorated with ostentatious decorations, but they seemed cold and uninviting. Yet I have visited the most humble of residences that have immersed me with the warmth and Spirit of the Lord, whose love permeated the place. That is what I want for my own home, and I know that it will come as a result of the worship of the Lord in that place. Only He can change an entire environment. An encounter with God should change the way we worship.

Mary, Martha, and Lazarus all changed because of an encounter with Jesus. They no longer served Him in the same way; they no longer had a mediocre relationship with Him; and they never worshipped Him in the same way. They had been changed.

81

Obstacles to

TRANSFORMATION

Ezra 1—4

CHAPTER SIX

Living in
SLAVERY

WHILE GOD WANTS US to be like Lazarus, free and raised to walk in the newness of life, the devil wants us to stay in bondage to our old selves and our old ways. Our spiritual adversary is working to resist us every step of the way. Anyone who asks me to autograph one of my books will find that after my signature I write Galatians 5:1. This is my life verse: "It is for freedom that Christ has set us free. Stand firm, then, and do not let yourselves be burdened again by a yoke of slavery." Are you . . .

in bondage to your schedule

in bondage to that relationship

in bondage to your career

in bondage to your habit

in bondage to your addiction

in bondage to your debt

in bondage to your fear

in bondage to your guilt?

Jesus wants to be the Lord of all you do, and if you invite Him, He will show you what an abundant, free life really looks like.

Abundant Liberty

He has broken your shackles and thrown them away, so why are you living as if you are still bound in some way? You are free to dance! In 1863, the Emancipation Proclamation was signed, sealed, and delivered in the United States of America. African slaves all over the nation were excited about the fact that they finally had the legal right to be free. Surprisingly, however, not all of the slaves responded the same way to this new decree.

First, some of the African slaves were so exhilarated about emancipation that they packed their bags immediately and left their masters. They were ready to go and experience freedom for all that it was worth. They were willing to risk everything because they believed that freedom was worth it! In fact, many slaves would rather have risked their lives for freedom than remain safe under the covering of their masters. That's how delighted this first group was to experience the newfound joy of freedom.

The second group of slaves included those who most often worked in the house with the master. They were treated better than all of the other slaves in every way. Household servants' lives were often much easier than the lives of the field workers. They became comfortable with their circumstances, and when they got the news about the Emancipation Proclamation, they weren't sure they wanted to risk that comfort to go experience freedom. They treasured the security of their current lifestyle over the price they would pay to be free. After all, life was pretty good in the house with their master. Freedom came with no promises and no guarantees. Yes, they would be free, but they would not be guaranteed a meal or shelter. They weren't sure freedom was worth that risk, so many slaves willingly chose to stay in slavery.

The third group is the most surprising of all. In my home state of Texas, we celebrate June 19th, or "Juneteenth." This is the anniversary of the day that the Emancipation Proclamation reached Texas. It wasn't until June 19, 1865, two years after the new law had been handed down, that slaves in Texas got the news of their legal freedom! For two whole years, the slaves in Texas were living in slavery, even though they legally had the right to freedom. Why? Some plantation owners in Texas had gotten together and conspired to conceal the news of the Proclamation. They knew that their farms and plantations would be hit hard if they lost all of their slaves, and they wanted to do everything they could to keep their work force intact. So for two years, the slaves in Texas lived in bondage with no knowledge that they had been set free!

Free at Last

Two thousand years ago there was an emancipation proclamation declared on your life! If you have been washed in the blood of Christ, then you are spiritually free. Which category of the emancipated Christian are you? Have you grabbed your freedom with two hands? Are you running full speed ahead and living the victorious Christian life? Yes, I know that it is costly and that you may have to make some sacrifices to live in complete freedom, but is it worth it to you? Are you determined not to allow the things of this world to hold you captive and keep you from experiencing the fullness of freedom in Christ? Those of us who not only accept the blood of Jesus as our eternal emancipation but also walk as free men and women right now will find that we experience the abundant life that Christ has to offer.

Maybe you fall into the second category. Maybe you have accepted the Lord but you refuse to walk as a free person because you are too comfortable where you are. You have become so used to the seemingly secure home of your former master, Satan, that you are not willing to risk losing that life of ease. Taking a risk for freedom may not look as inviting as your current level of comfort. Sometimes we find ourselves so entangled in sin, disobedience, or simply the goods of this temporary world, that when freedom comes, we let it pass us by. We are so accustomed to living in bondage by internal chains of guilt, shame, and fear or by material chains of possessions, homes, money, success, and other needless attachments. We are not really interested in the victorious Christian life as long as we can just get by with what we have. We are glad that we are saved, but our rebellious nature has not allowed us to move past what is comfortable to what is spiritually profitable. We know that we can live in freedom if we choose to, but we prefer not to do so. The price is just too high.

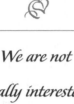

We are not really interested in the victorious Christian life as long as we can just get by with what we have.

Or perhaps you see yourself in the third category. Are you saved, but you haven't received the news in your heart that you have the right to live as a free person? Those of us in this group don't know that there is more to the blood of Jesus than just grace to be saved; there is grace to live in abundant freedom. Satan, our former master, doesn't want us to know that the eternal emancipation proclamation has been given final approval and is pertinent to us. Satan will do anything to keep his workforce intact. If he can keep you from getting this life-transforming information, then you will keep serving him. You will continue to work for his kingdom and for his purposes because you won't recognize that you have the spiritual right to be free. It is time, my friend, for you to know that you have been emancipated. If there is no other reason that you are reading this book other than to get this one message, then so be it. *You are free!* You have been . . .

emancipated from the need for earthly treasures

emancipated from keeping up with the Joneses

emancipated from your addiction

emancipated from that broken heart

emancipated from the guilt of your past

emancipated from that bad habit

emancipated from that relationship

emancipated from fear

emancipated from guilt.

If we didn't have these things to worry about what would we think about?

What are the chains that bind you? You do not have to be enslaved by them anymore. Thank God, you can be free! Now all you have to do is just put one foot in front of the other and begin to walk in liberty. Give the Lord complete control over your particular area of bondage. Tell Him that you are ready to be loosed of the chains that entangle you so that you can move forward. Freedom comes when we make Him the Lord of our lives. It is easy for us to call Him "Lord," but to live under His lordship means we willingly submit every area of our lives to His control. Jesus wants to be . . .

"It is for freedom that Christ has set us free" (Galatians 5:1).

the Lord of your relationships

the Lord of your career

the Lord of your home

the Lord of your eating

the Lord of your heart

the Lord of your mind

the Lord of your past, present, and future.

Not quite sure how to live free or in freedom

89

Ask the Lord to show you into which category of the emancipated Christian you fall. You don't have to walk as the world walks—bound by every imaginable habit, addiction, and fear. You have been changed.

Like the Auca Indian who is called "Grandfather" by the children of the ones he murdered, so you are no longer a savage either. You have been called to be different. How dare we choose to be in bondage to the very things from which He freed us with His shed blood! This very day, you don't have to be bound anymore. You aren't a slave. You are a free person! In fact, you have been granted freedom on a silver platter. You don't have to earn it. All you have to do is accept the gift. I know that it seems risky, that you may feel you have a lot to lose, but freedom is worth it. You will never know the abundance awaiting you unless you put your fears aside and move forward. God has given you full access to a life of freedom, so live it!

Satan is keeping the chains of your particular area of captivity on you and is trying to prevent you from experiencing the abundant life that God has planned for you. Satan is telling you that you don't deserve it or that you can never have it. He wants you to live a mediocre Christian life by choosing to remain a part of the norm instead of stepping apart and away from the crowd as you live a transformed life. As long as you are bound by the deceiver and living the life of a slave, then Satan has you in the palm of his hand. He will use any scheme to get you where he wants you to be. Distraction, discouragement, deception —these are his tried-and-true methods for creating obstacles to our transformation. Don't give him the satisfaction. *Walk in freedom!*

CHAPTER SEVEN

The Danger of DISTRACTIONS

THROUGHOUT THE ENTIRE Old Testament, God was calling His people back to Himself after they had chosen their own way over His way. The children of Israel encountered His holiness and supernatural power on many occasions, yet they continued to go their own way. Scripture gives very specific reasons why the Israelites repeatedly disobeyed God's call. Satan uses the same tools today to keep you and me from passionately pursuing God's will. If we can recognize these things and ask God to remove the power that they have over us, then we can get busy doing the King's work.

God loved His people and had proven this love on numerous occasions. He delivered them from Pharaoh, spared the lives of their firstborn sons, parted the Red Sea, fought on their behalf in battle, and continually protected them from their enemies. As if that weren't enough, He also fed them with manna, quenched their thirst with water from a rock, took them to the Promised Land, and repeatedly forgave their sins. Still, they often failed to recognize the power of God, despite their many encounters with Him. They refused to change. They continued to go their own way, loudly complaining against God's unfair treatment of them and neglecting God's commands altogether.

We too have had marvelous encounters with God time and time again but have failed to recognize them.

Sound familiar? We are just like the children of Israel; we too have had marvelous encounters with God time and time again but have failed to recognize them. "What encounters?" you might ask. Often we don't recognize events in our lives as encounters with God. When things go well for us, we like to think that "our hard work has finally paid off." Or we figure we're "just lucky." However, we must recognize that "every good and perfect gift is from above" (James 1:17). There is absolutely nothing that you and I do for ourselves. God is the Source of all things—even the very breath that you draw in. Don't miss the smallest encounters with God. The fact that your marriage has been salvaged, child saved, life spared, finances taken care of; or body healed is no small thing and had nothing to do with you or your ability. He deserves the recognition for even those things that we take for granted. The Israelites trusted in their own abilities rather than recognizing that, had it not been for supernatural interventions by the Lord, their lives would have been drastically different.

By some stretch of our imagination, we come to believe that we've made it on our own. Yet just as God intervened in the Israelites' lives, so He also breaks into our lives. Look at the similarities in our stories. If you are saved, then you are only saved because He has called you unto Himself. If you have been freed from some overwhelming bondage in your life, then it is because He ordered your release from that "Pharaoh." If you have children, then you have seen the goodness of God in sparing their lives. If He has ever cleared away murky waters in your finances, health, marriage, or another aspect of your life and has allowed you to walk safely through a terrible situation on dry ground, then His hand divided the Red Sea for you.

If you have ever been in the midst of a contentious, irresolvable situation with your spouse or boss but somehow everything worked out fine, then God was the one fighting your battle. If you know where your next meal is coming from, then it is because He feeds you from His right hand with miraculous manna from above and water from rocks. If, after years of struggle, you have come to a place of rest and peace in your life, then it is only because He has led you to the Promised Land. If, like me, you are a sinner in need of grace, then He miraculously forgives your sin! Encounters with a transforming God are happening all around you. Are you missing them?

Although the children of Israel experienced numerous encounters with God, they still seemed more consumed with their desires than with the Lord's. True spiritual transformation begins when we are willing to relinquish control of what we want. Then God is able to give us what He wants, and what He wants for us will most assuredly be better than anything we could think up on our own. The Israelites were never quite willing to believe that, so it took them a long time to experience what God wanted and to walk in the freedom He had so graciously granted them.

> *True spiritual transformation begins when we are willing to relinquish control of what we want.*

The Consequences of Disobedience

Because of Israel's continued disobedience, the Lord reluctantly gave them over to what they wanted and let them face the consequences of their selfishness. He allowed the Babylonians, ruled by Nebuchadnezzar, to come in and destroy everything that they knew and loved dearly.

The LORD, the God of their fathers, sent word to them through his messengers again and again. . . . But they mocked God's messengers, despised his words and scoffed at his prophets until the wrath of the LORD was aroused against his people and there was no remedy. He brought up against them the king of the Babylonians, who killed their young men with the sword in the sanctuary, and spared neither young man nor young woman, old man or aged. God handed all of them over to Nebuchadnezzar. . . . They set fire to God's temple and broke down the wall of Jerusalem; they burned all the palaces and destroyed everything of value there.

He carried into exile to Babylon the remnant, who escaped from the sword, and they became servants to him and his sons until the kingdom of Persia came to power.

2 Chronicles 36:15–20

For seventy years the remnant of Jews was separated from everything that they treasured. The Babylonians demolished everything that was dear to Israel, including the city wall, which protected them physically, and the temple, which protected them spiritually. The most tragic and painful part of this destruction was the desecration of the temple. Their spiritual house was not like our churches today. We go on Sundays, sometimes Wednesday nights for Bible study, and perhaps other times during the week for a meeting. To the Jews, the temple meant everything. All of the banking, all of the economy, and all of the worship took place there. Their livelihood was tied up in the temple. It was their foundation and the soul of their nation—the symbol of their covenant with the God who had chosen them. However, they were unable to rebuild it because they were in exile in a foreign land for seventy years.

The book of Ezra picks up the continuing saga of the love relationship between God and His chosen people. After those seventy years of captivity, the Persians conquered the Babylonians, and Ezra begins by telling us that King Cyrus of Persia was now on the throne. Once again the Lord intervened on behalf of His people, and yet another encounter with God began for the children of Israel. Here was another opportunity for the Israelites to recognize the glory of the Most High and choose to change.

This encounter began when the Lord stirred King Cyrus's heart to send out a written proclamation to all of his kingdom saying, "Anyone of his people among you—may his God be with him, and let him go up to Jerusalem in Judah and build the temple of the LORD, the God of Israel, the God who is in Jerusalem" (Ezra 1:3). King Cyrus declared freedom to all of the captives of the past seventy years and gave them the option to return to their home in Jerusalem.

Take note of why the king released them. They were freed for the sole purpose of rebuilding the temple of the Lord. Once again, God was giving His people the opportunity to get their priorities straight—to stop doing what had become important to them in captivity and get busy doing what was important to God. Naturally they were ready and anxious to go, right? No! An encounter with God *should* always transform our priorities.

The Distraction of Comfort

King Cyrus's proclamation was to all of the Jews in his kingdom. Yet in the end, only the tribes of Judah and Benjamin, with a few members of other tribes, decided to go back to Judah and rebuild the house of the Lord. The number of people who returned to Judah reached approximately forty-nine thousand. That may sound like a large number, but if you compare it to the hundreds of thousands in captivity, it no longer seems so large. Consider this: Of the twelve tribes of Israel that had the option of going back, only two tribes went. Twelve tribes of Israel received the same proclamation of freedom from the same king, but only two took the king up on his offer. Ten chose willingly to stay behind in a foreign land, bound by their captors. Their reasoning was simple: They had accumulated wealth and the comfort that it brings and did not want to leave that behind. They succumbed to the distractions of life in Babylon.

Lord Foulgrin's Letters, a fictional book by Randy Alcorn, sheds light on the schemes of the devil. Inspired by C. S. Lewis's *The Screwtape Letters*, Alcorn's book describes how the devil uses various "tools of distraction" to keep us from doing what God wants. It is the story of a man named Fletcher. Lord Foulgrin, one of Satan's demons, writes letters of advice and direction to a demon named Squaltaint who is responsible for preventing Fletcher from coming to know the Lord, whom they call the Enemy. In one of the letters to Squaltaint, Lord Foulgrin says, "Your job is to help Fletcher move impulsively to fill his emptiness with all the things the Enemy forbids. These have value not simply because they'll destroy him, but because they'll distract him. In the final analysis, distraction from the Enemy is all we need to accomplish. . . . Use television, computer, telephone, newspaper, sports events, work—anything and everything to distract him from self-evaluation. Why do you suppose technology and media exist but as tools for distraction?"

Squaltaint's job was simply to distract. How many tools of distraction has the devil strategically planted in your life so that you don't have enough time to put first things first? Are you an Internet junkie? Are you an e-mail-aholic? Or is it a specific television show that keeps you so captivated that you just don't have time for what is most important? In the final analysis, distraction from God, regardless of the means, is all that Satan needs to accomplish. If he can distract us by the things that we have, then he will succeed in keeping us from the things of God.

It's not that we intentionally rebel; it's that we are just so caught up in all that we have that we never get around to what God has for us.

The children of Israel didn't intend to permanently settle in Babylon. However, over time, life in Babylon distracted them from God's plans for them. I'm sure they may have intended to go back someday, but after years of captivity, returning to Jerusalem became less and less of a priority. "What's one more year in Babylon going to hurt?" they may have asked themselves. In the same way, we often have good intentions, but they rarely become priorities. We may intend to have a quiet time, yet neglect to prioritize it on our list of things to do each day. We hope to get around to witnessing to our neighbor, but we tell ourselves, "What's one more day of putting it off?" We intend to change our ways someday, but because change is not a priority to us, we are left with only good intentions.

What rebuilding project is the Lord asking you to undertake right now?

In God's economy, we are successful when we lay aside the things of this world and immediately accomplish what He has asked us to do. The rewards of doing so will be eternal pleasures for you! In Israel's case, the Lord gave them specific instructions to rebuild the temple. What rebuilding project is the Lord asking you to undertake right now? Are you too distracted to give yourself fully to that work?

King Cyrus went on to say in his proclamation that "the people of any place where survivors may now be living are to provide [those Jews who return to Jerusalem] with silver and gold, with goods and livestock, and with freewill offerings for the temple of God in Jerusalem" (Ezra 1:4). Many of the Jewish people apparently liked the idea of supporting the project rather than actually being involved in it. The king asked those ten tribes of Israel that stayed behind in the Persian Empire to utilize their financial resources to support the building project in Judah. They were *contributors* to the plan and will of God, but they were not active *participants*.

Are you a

contributor

or a

participant?

Let me ask you, are you a contributor or a participant? In 1 Corinthians 15:58, Paul says, "Therefore, my dear brothers, stand firm. Let nothing move you. Always give yourselves fully to the work of the Lord, because you know that your labor in the Lord is not in vain." Many Christians who desire to obtain and sustain their treasures find themselves in a spiritual trap, and they are often on the outskirts of the will and favor of God. They are looking on, applauding, and even contributing their resources to what God is doing, but they are not active participants in the process. Therefore, they don't reap the same rewards as those who are willing to sacrifice and rebuild the house.

What is your position in the work of the Lord? If He has called you to teach, get up and start teaching. It doesn't matter how ill equipped you feel you may be. If He has called you, He will equip you. If He has called you to finance a ministry, give wholeheartedly, holding nothing back. Maybe the "temple" He has called you to build demands that you give yourself completely to serving your husband and children instead of spending your days at the office.

Are you comfortable just cheering for those who are working for God and watching them receive His favor, or are you the one whom God can trust to be an active participant in the building of His kingdom? Only those who pack their bags and move toward freedom, no matter what the cost, will reap the benefits that only come from being in the will of God.

The Distraction of Materialism

Some of the Israelites willingly chose a life of captivity in a foreign land over a life of freedom in their homeland. After seventy years, why would they want to stay in Babylon? The answer is simple: they were distracted by the sin of materialism.

Of this emigration to Judah, the *Commentary Critical and Explanatory on the Whole Bible* (by Robert Jamieson, A. R. Fausset, and David Brown) writes that those "who retained their attachment to the pure worship of God naturally took the lead in this movement. Their example was followed by all whose piety and patriotism were strong enough to brave the various discouragements attending the enterprise. They were liberally assisted by multitudes of their captive countrymen, who, born in Babylonia or comfortably established in it by family connections or the possession of property, chose to remain."

We must remember that Jerusalem's desolation and Israel's exile lasted seventy years. That is a long time! They had accrued wealth, possessions, land, and social status. They were comfortable. They had not just scrounged to survive but had made homes for themselves, settled their families, had children and grandchildren, and joined society in their nation of exile. They had done pretty well in Babylon these past seventy years. Many of them preferred to stay in a foreign land with the comfort that they treasured rather than experience freedom in the land of God's promise.

Apparently that foreign land didn't feel so foreign to them anymore. The change that God wanted to bring to their lives by bringing them home meant risking the loss of all of their material possessions. Since the journey to Jerusalem would mean traveling on foot, they were going to have to leave behind most of what they had accumulated. And what they did bring with them, they would risk losing along the way to thieves who preyed on travelers. Ten of the tribes of Israel weren't willing to risk the loss of their earthly possessions. However, the tribes of Benjamin and Judah were willing to put everything on the line, even their wealth, to follow God's plan. *Do you think these were poorer tribes?*

Most of us are often so caught up in the stuff that we have that we would rather stay in captivity with our possessions than risk them to

Most of us would rather stay in captivity with our possessions than risk them to pursue the things of God.

pursue the things of God. Perhaps for you, the call of God has already come to move you out of corporate America and into ministry, but you hesitate, knowing what that might mean to your pocketbook. God has called many new moms out of the workplace and back home with their children, resulting in the loss of the corporate status they have worked diligently to obtain. Or perhaps the Lord is asking you to relinquish a relationship. You continue to hold on tightly to what you want, while all the while you are missing out on the beautiful freedom that the will of God would have for you. What so-called "treasures" do you need to rid your life of so that the Lord can replace them with what is truly valuable?

The Giver of all good things blesses us so much, but we often forget the Giver and worship the gifts! When you encounter God and He clearly shows you what He wants you to do, do your possessions or the comforts that you treasure still hold you captive? Are you so caught up in your many material blessings that you forget your first allegiance to God alone? An encounter with God should cause us to adjust the value that we place on our earthly possessions. No material thing—whether person or product, habit or lifestyle—should ever stand in the way of our doing what the Lord has called us to do. Are we, like the children of Israel, willing to stay in a state of captivity in our lives just to keep a hand on the earthly things that we treasure?

What you are willing and unwilling to do with your earthly possessions is a direct indication of your relationship with and love for God. In Matthew 6:21, Jesus said, "Where your treasure is, there your heart will be also." In other words, where we spend our time, money, and energy are direct indications of what we value the most. Are your treasures stored up in earthly or heavenly places? This will indicate to you where your relationship with God really lies.

Chuck Swindoll, noted author and pastor, often tells the story of meeting Corrie ten Boom, a Christian woman who survived the Nazi death camps in World War II. Dr. Swindoll was trudging through a time in his life when things weren't going well personally. He says that this woman, little in stature but enormous in faith, walked up to him, cupped her little hands underneath his bigger hands, and said, "Chuck, whatever you treasure in life, hold it very loosely so that it doesn't hurt when God has to pry your fingers open to take it away."

My friend, whatever you treasure in life—your kids, your marriage, the money you have made, the car you are driving, or the lifestyle that God has blessed you with—remember to hold it loosely so that it doesn't hurt when God has to pry your fingers open to take it away. Don't clutch it tightly. Always remember that your possessions are not truly yours. God gives them to us on loan to manage until He comes again.

The Root Problem

If you read between the lines, you will see the real reason the people of Israel did not go back to Jerusalem to rebuild the temple. The Jews had become accustomed to the hedonistic society in which they had lived for seventy years in Babylon. The stench of humanism (the love of self) permeated the air and dictated every step they took.

As a result of the long years that they had spent there, selfishness and pride (where materialism has its roots) consumed them. The Jews had become selfish by holding on too tightly to their possessions, unwilling to release them at God's request; they became prideful by thinking highly of their ability to obtain for themselves rather than trusting what God could give them. These two underminers of the faith, selfishness and pride, steered the people in the wrong direction. As a result, many missed the fulfillment that only obedience to the Lord can provide.

> *"The Lord does not look at the things man looks at. Man looks at the outward appearance, but the Lord looks at the heart"* (1 Samuel 16:7).

The real problem with materialism is internal; it simply evidences itself in an external manner, such as an obsession with clothes, money, and material things. When God is pruning away external treasure, it is most likely because He is trying to attack an internal problem. He is not necessarily interested in the material possessions that you have acquired in life. He has no hard feelings against them until you begin to cling to them. If you have accumulated wealth, then enjoy it as a gift from the Lord. The problem comes if those things keep you from accomplishing the things He has called you to do for His kingdom.

Today, even our secular counterparts have begun to call into question the seemingly never-ending rat race to acquire more things. They're complaining about the effect that this is having on their personal and family lives.

Former Secretary of Labor Robert Reich left his influential position in the Clinton cabinet because he wanted to spend more time with his family. Reich observed that America has a new definition of success, and from all indications, he had seemingly achieved it in every way. Yet he found that work had taken over his life, and he wasn't satisfied living chained to his job. "The more money you make, very often the longer hours you're putting in," Reich stated. "We've gotten to the point where even though we are very prosperous overall as a nation, we are remarkably poor in terms of the quality of our lives outside work" (*American Way Magazine*, February 2001). A man in one of the most powerful, prestigious positions in America voiced sentiments quite similar to those of King Solomon in Ecclesiastes 2:11: "Yet when I surveyed all that my hands had done and what I had toiled to achieve, everything was meaningless, a chasing after the wind; nothing was gained under the sun."

Our lives have become like a rat race where the participants frantically claw to impede each other's progress in hopes to cross the finish line first. Yet there is no finish line! Just when you think you have accomplished something of lasting value and excellence, the standard of excellence has changed; then you have to continue to strive toward the goal of the new ideal in order to be a success. The standard of excellence in our society is an ever-changing measure that we cannot afford to maintain.

One Christmas, I shopped for a PlayStation for my husband. After driving all over Dallas to stores that were sold out of this highly desired commodity, I was thrilled when I finally found one available. I was so proud on our first Christmas day as a married couple to see my husband tear away the paper and beam like a giddy child. However, in only nine short months, I started seeing advertisements for the "new and improved" PlayStation II that did immeasurably more than the model I had purchased. I was amazed to see that just when I thought I had the best, the definition of "best" changed within a matter of months!

Isn't that the norm with most material things? Each year car companies create new models, the fashion industry designs new styles, furniture companies offer new selections, and the list goes on and on. This is why it is so important that we not focus on the world to measure our rate of success. Does the world really know what success means? It has set up its own standard, but that standard is not similar in any way to the standards of Scripture. I have found only one standard that is the same yesterday, today, and forever. His name is Jesus.

When we meet with God, the things that used to be important to us should become dim and meaningless in the presence of One so grand. His will for us should always supersede what we desire for ourselves. The will of God is the only place where we can discover true freedom in this life. This means that our priorities must be changed. We must not let anything get in the way of our focus on what the Lord asks us to do.

CHAPTER EIGHT

The Cost of
TRANSFORMATION

But many of the older priests and Levites and family heads, who had seen the former temple, wept aloud when they saw the foundation of this temple being laid, while many others shouted for joy.

Ezra 3:12

THE JEWS WHO STAYED behind in Babylon were not willing to pay the price of transformation and freedom. However, those who went ahead to Jerusalem soon discovered that the price was more than they were willing to pay, too. Sixteen years elapsed after they returned to the city, and the temple, though it had a new foundation, still lay in ruins.

After they initially laid the foundation for the temple, the work ceased. They discovered that living as a changed people was going to be more costly than they had expected. They found it difficult to prioritize the construction of God's temple over securing their own comforts. Not only that, but they also compared the little work they did manage to do on the temple to the former glory of the original temple. They felt that they didn't measure up, so they got discouraged. Other people taunted them, and they had to deal with criticism. What had once looked so appealing was turning out to be a difficult task.

Like them, we often grow discouraged when we realize the price of change. We often get revved up for our lives to be different; yet weeks, months, even years later, we look around, and so little has changed. We say we ought to be changed because of our encounter with God, but we often remain stunted in our old habits and old ways. This is because change is costly.

"This is to my Father's glory, that you bear much fruit, show-ing yourselves to be my disciples" (John 15:8).

The Process of Pruning

The painful process of allowing God to pull away those things that are keeping you from His best is called "pruning." Jesus describes this process in John 15:1–2: "I am the true vine, and my Father is the gardener. He cuts off every branch in me that bears no fruit, while every branch that does bear fruit he prunes so that it will be even more fruitful." His goal for your life is not that you have the most incred-ible clothes or live in a fabulous house. Those things may be your desires, but His desire is for us to be fruitful.

If you feel the Lord tugging away some of the stuff in your life and pushing you toward a life that is free, it is not because He is trying to hurt you. He may be pruning away the areas in your life that are keeping you from producing the most fruit for His kingdom. Sometimes that means cutting away dead branches, but often it means cutting off perfectly healthy branches and stalks to encourage new growth. God, the Master Gardener, prunes areas of our lives so that we can grow. Pruning hurts, but it promotes new life. Our possessions and lifestyles often have such a grip on us that we forget the priorities to which God has called us. God is determined to strip those things away.

I know that change may sound scary, because for some it may mean taking a pay cut to do what God wants you to do. It may mean that you will have to put yourself out there emotionally in your marriage and give more than you ever have. It may be hard for you to extend yourself to that drug-addicted family member and let him know that you love him. It may be hard to break off that relationship from which you know the Lord wants you to be free. Or it may mean not depending so much on your earthly position and status. Regardless of the form of sacrifice the Lord asks of you, being a follower of Christ always means taking up your cross daily to follow Him.

Taking up a cross wasn't easy for Christ, and it will not be easy for us. But it will be worth it. Hebrews 12:2 says that Jesus, "for the joy set before him endured the cross." He wasn't looking at the cross; He was looking *beyond* the cross to the joy that would follow! If freedom in God's will for you means that you are in the path of a cross, shift your vision to *just beyond it,* to the illuminating joy that will follow. The will of God is the only place where you will find true peace, meaning, and joy in your life. It is the only place where you can produce abundant fruit.

The will of God is the only place where you will find true peace, meaning, and joy in your life.

That is precisely what was taking place in the lives of the Israelites when they returned to Jerusalem. The pruning process that had begun when they were exiles in Babylon now continued into their new beginnings in Jerusalem. God wanted to strip away all of those things that were keeping His people from putting first things first.

Pruning Our Selfishness

When the two tribes left Babylon and went back to Judah, they carried the root issue of materialism with them—selfishness. They began feeding their starved desires for the comforts of home before they attended to God's house. Although they were willing to go to Judah, they procrastinated on God's priority—rebuilding the temple. Instead, they focused on their own needs. Ten tribes of Israel wanted to stay in Babylon because they didn't want to leave their possessions and their comfort zone. They wanted the wealth that they had accumulated in captivity and didn't want to risk losing it in order to obtain freedom. That same selfishness also consumed the two tribes of Israel that did return to Judah. They wanted to obtain earthly resources and put aside the priorities of their true King. This is a reminder that all of us, no matter how willing we seem to obey God, are potential victims to the disease of materialism that plagues our humanity.

One of my favorite books in the Bible, Haggai, picks up sixteen years after the initial group of Israelites had returned to Jerusalem to begin the process of rebuilding. God sent the prophet Haggai to His children to spur them to remember that their sole purpose in coming back to the city was to reconstruct the temple. In Haggai 1:2, 4, the Lord says, "These people say, 'The time has not yet come for the LORD's house to be built.' . . . Is it a time for you yourselves to be living in your paneled houses, while this house remains a ruin?"

They had the energy and financial resources to build God's house but were too busy using those things to build their own houses. And not just any kind of houses—they were living in "paneled houses." This suggests that these weren't your ordinary, modest dwelling places. The people spent time and paid attention to detail in their valuable homes. They were ornately decorated and lavishly filled. God's concern was not simply that they had taken time and energy to build shelter for themselves and their families and had seen to their immediate needs; God

We need to ask for our needs—not our wants

was troubled that they allowed their wants and obvious selfish desires to take precedence over the work of God. These folks were chillin' in the suburbs in lavishly decorated homes while God's house was in the middle of the city, still lying desolate!

> *Some of us are so wrapped up in what we want that we neglect what God wants for us.*

Some of us are so wrapped up in what we want that we neglect what God wants for us. We are too busy using our resources, not just to build our own houses, but also to decorate and redecorate them. We often maintain a standard of living that leaves us with few resources to invest in the kingdom of God. What "temple" are you building at the expense of the Lord's? This does not give evidence of a transformed life. Are you willing to miss the beauty of freedom in the will of God because of the attachment that you have to the many blessings God has allowed you to have?

As a young married woman, I have seen this principle of pruning most evident in the area of my time, and that pruning can really hurt. When I was single, I was in charge of my life's schedule. I was the one who decided what I would eat, where I would go, what speaking engagements I would take, and how I would spend my money and my time. Now that I am married with a small child, I am going through the process of allowing God to prune away the selfishness and pride that often accompanies the single life. Married people often say, "You don't know how selfish you are until you are married." I certainly have seen that to be the case! I was so used to doing things my way and being concerned with my career and ministry that it was tough for me to relinquish that objective now that I have a family.

Sowing Deep

My friend Tammy Maltby is a gorgeous, bouncy little woman who is outgoing and personable and loves the Lord. She has been a true example to me through word and deed when it comes to the principle of putting first things first. When Tammy and her husband had been married only six months, they were surprised to find out that she was pregnant. Though they had always wanted children, they had hoped for more time alone before stepping into parenthood. She soon gave birth to a beautiful daughter named Mackenzie. A few years later, they adopted their son Samuel from Korea, and Tammy felt that their family was complete. She longed to move back into a career that would use her creativity (instead of just wiping little derrières all day)! Yet when Sam was only a year old, Tammy's husband felt strongly that they should consider adopting an older, special-needs child from Russia. Tammy said that the idea nearly put her under—three children under the age of four and a husband who traveled more than 250 days a year would mean many days and nights of isolation and loneliness. God was certainly pruning her heart!

During the process of adopting their Russian-born daughter, Tatiana, Tammy discovered that she was pregnant with their fourth child! Now they would have four children under the age of five, one of whom spoke no English and had never lived in anything but an orphanage.

Tammy went from being a jet-setting, footloose, single adult at twenty-five to being a stay-at-home mother of four at thirty! Life changed drastically for her, and selfishness and pride had to take a back seat—and quickly. The pruning process was in full swing. Tammy made the difficult choice to put everything aside for ten years to do what the Lord was asking of her and to focus on being a mom. There were many offers for her to pursue different career opportunities, but she decided that this was the season for her to sow deep into the lives of her husband and children.

> *True beauty comes from the deep and often painful pruning of our hopes, dreams, and desires.*

Although she was terribly lonely during those ten years, she learned in that house full of needs the mystery that true beauty comes from the deep and often painful pruning of our hopes, dreams, and desires. She came to trust and understand that real beauty is born when we give away our lives for the sake of others.

Now at forty-two, Tammy is a television host and author of a book called *Lifegiving: Discovering the Secrets to a Beautiful Life*; but her full-time job is her active involvement in her children's lives. She has a beautiful home, an abundant life, a family who adores her, and a great love for the Lord. Her life looks, feels, and smells like a wonderful fairytale! Yet her life is fruitful now only because she willingly went through the pruning process earlier.

Although it was painful, Tammy allowed God to prune her life so that she could see the fruit in due season. And by bearing that fruit, she has blessed many other people's lives. To meet her is to come face-to-face with a well-seasoned woman to whom God has shown favor because of her resistance to pride and selfishness in her resources and time. Even though it was hard and frustrating to let go of so many of her life's loves for that season, she submitted to God's pruning and encourages me to do the same. Her advice to me has been, "Priscilla, sow into your husband and your children. Lay aside anything that hinders you from doing so. You will be glad and far richer as a result." Tammy's life and lifegiving message attest to that truth. We reap future fruit by sowing selflessly now.

Don't allow selfishness to keep you from experiencing all that God has planned for you. Trust me, what He has planned is fantastic—better than anything that you could create with your own two hands! The question is whether or not you and I are willing to get rid of what we want to make room for what He wants, even if only for a season. There may be a season in your life when you are not doing all that you thought you would do in your career. It may mean that you cannot afford the home you have always desired since you will be staying home with your kids instead of bringing in a second income. It may mean the ministry that you were so excited about starting at your church may have to wait so you can take care of your ministry at home to your husband and children. It may mean sacrificing the time that you would have spent with friends so that you can make time to spend alone with God. As a single woman, it may mean putting dates with potential mates on hold so you can concentrate on what God is doing in this season of your life. Ask the Lord to reveal what His priorities are for you right now, and then get busy being obedient. Future fruit is always the result of present obedience.

Future fruit is always the result of present obedience.

Satan is subtle in his deception. He strategically blinds us with the sin of our pride and makes sure we call it self-assuredness. He veils our spiritual eyesight and makes us see our sin of selfishness as self-interest. He reminds us that no one else will look out for our interests, so we must take care of ourselves—right? Surely there is nothing wrong with that! Satan always tries to get us to disregard sin and excuse it as a bad habit or just human nature. Let's ask the Lord to reveal our patterns of selfishness so that we can remove them from our lives and move on to rebuilding the temple. It is in this building process that we will find true fulfillment.

Pruning Our Security

God not only cuts away selfishness, but He also whittles away any trace of your reliance on your earthly position or status. When Israel returned from Babylon, nothing was the same anymore. They could not point to a beautiful city to call home. They were basically nomads without any earthly security. They had to rely fully on God.

I have taken the advice of my friend Tammy and other godly women by asking the Lord what He wants me to cut away from my life so I can pursue Him wholeheartedly. As I prepared to write this book, the Lord convicted me about several areas of my life that I need to release. He allowed me to see clearly several hindrances to my life and ministry, and He began to prune away those things.

It has been a painful experience for me to let go of many of these things, yet the most meaningful, albeit painful, thing has been the release of my name. On the cover of my first book, *A Jewel in His Crown*, my name is written "Priscilla Evans Shirer." On all of my tapes and brochures, my name is written that same way. When I got married, my husband and I agreed that in my ministry I would keep and use my maiden name. Our compromise on this was that I would use "Evans" for business purposes only, and on personal and legal documents I would use my middle name and married name.

This plan seemed to be a good one, except that it became increasingly hard to find the dividing line between business and personal. My life *is* my ministry. Many people kept calling me Priscilla Evans and even, at times, attached my maiden name to my husband. As you can imagine, this was not honoring to him. After almost two years of marriage, it hurt him to realize that many people still did not recognize me as *his* wife and *his* family. I could see how much this hurt him, but it was equally painful to me to give up the name "Evans." I kept telling my husband (and myself) that my reason for wanting to keep my maiden name was not a big deal. I really believed that my reason was simply my love for the heritage that the Lord had given me.

Then the Lord began to reveal the deeper reasons why I wanted to keep my maiden name, and most of those reasons were rooted in self-ishness and pride. I asked the Lord to show me what areas of my life I needed to give up. I first became convicted about my name because I realized how hard it would be for me to let it go. Even today, I struggle to exclude "Evans" from my signature or introduction. My difficulty in releasing this to the Lord indicated to me that there was a problem. The Holy Spirit showed me that I was indeed holding on too tightly to my name, which represented my history. He showed me that the issue was not my name at all; the issue was recognition.

My father, Tony Evans, is a very famous preacher. When people introduced me or spoke of me, I felt a certain sense of pride when I was recognized as his daughter. He is worth every ounce of praise that he gets, but my reason for wanting to be associated with him was to receive attention and recognition. When I spoke at conferences, I found that the audience received me better when they knew who my daddy was; they could make a mental association between him and me that endeared me to them. Acknowledging who my father is will often break the ice with an audience that might not be very familiar with me.

The Lord showed me that I have HIS name, and that is all I need.

Now there is no problem with people knowing that my father is Tony Evans. (I am extremely proud of that fact.) However, there is a problem with my depending on my name to do what only God can do. The Lord showed me that I have *His* name, and that is all I need. He uncovered a heaping pile of self-righteous-ness in my heart that I didn't even know existed. He showed me that I must surrender to Him my own attempts to receive recognition. Do you see? What He asked me to give up was something external, but the real issue was an internal one.

Not only did my sacrifice honor God, but it certainly honored my husband as well, and it allowed me to sow into my relationship with him. When I introduce myself as plain ol' Priscilla Shirer, perhaps no one will know that my daddy is Tony Evans, but I can sense the pride that my husband feels in knowing I belong to him. At first it was scary for me, and to be honest, it still is. But it sure is worth it!

Is the Lord trying to cut away your need for recognition, your love of money, your desire to succeed in the eyes of others, or some other hidden quality that people don't know about you? It will be scary to let these things go, but the result will blow you away!

Pruning Our Relationships

Ezra 4 tells us that disguised Samaritans, enemies of Judah, came to the leader of the temple building project, Zerubbabel, and asked if they could build alongside the Jews. They explained to Zerubbabel that they too worshipped the God of Israel and wanted to see the temple erected.

The worst enemies were those who came in the name of friendship.

They seemed to have the best interests of the Jewish community in mind. In fact, these enemies were "strangers, settled in the land of Israel" (Robert Jamieson, A. R. Fausset, and David Brown, *Commentary Critical and Explanatory on the Whole Bible*). In other words, these people lived, worked, and played right alongside the Jewish people. They had probably befriended them to some extent and now offered to help in the construction of the temple.

The people groups who seemed likely candidates for Israel's worst enemies were the

Chaldeans or the Persians, yet these groups welcomed the building project. The worst enemies of Judah and Benjamin were not the obvious ones—the Chaldeans or Persians. The worst enemies were those who came in the name of friendship—the Samaritans. These superstitious people served the God of Israel, but they also served other gods with equal fervor. They knew that the temple would be a major blow to their superstitious ways, so they set out to thwart the process.

However, Zerubbabel wisely saw through their superficial pretenses and, with great spiritual insight, retained complete control over the building process. No matter how helpful these people offered to be, no matter how friendly they seemed, something about them bothered Zerubbabel. He decided that, despite the well-rehearsed request, the people did not have anything in common with the children of Israel and that they should not build with them.

As kindly yet directly as he could, Zerubbabel told them, "You have no part with us in building a temple to our God. We alone will build it for the LORD, the God of Israel, as King Cyrus, the king of Persia, commanded us" (Ezra 4:3). Although the Samaritans claimed to follow the God of Israel, they did not seek Him exclusively. This disparity between wholehearted worship and divided loyalties was enough for Zerubbabel to ban this group from participating as co-laborers in the building project.

The Samaritans responded in anger. They "set out to discourage the people of Judah and make them afraid to go on building. They hired counselors to work against them and frustrate their plans during the entire reign of Cyrus king of Persia and down to the reign of Darius king of Persia" (Ezra 4:4–5). Since they did not have the power to take the Israelites by force, they did everything else in their power to thwart their project. These people who had so recently claimed that they wanted to help even went as far as writing letters to the king, encouraging him to halt the construction. For approximately twenty years the

116

building process came to a screeching halt because these people, disguised as friends with common interests, were in actuality the enemy.

Redefining Friendship

After a transforming encounter with God, you and I should always choose carefully the people in our close circle of friends. We must keep close tabs on the company we choose to keep. Are there any people in your life who look like your friends but are actually on the side of the enemy? Is there a person you are dating right now or a friend you spend time with who is not fully in line with what God is doing in your life? People who are not *for* what God is doing in you, no matter how friendly they appear, are ultimately *against* what He is doing.

Proverbs 27:17 says, "As iron sharpens iron, so one man sharpens another." Are the people with whom you surround yourself sharpening you or dulling you? Are they pointing you toward God or away from God? They *are* doing one or the other; we can't help but influence and be influenced by our friends. We must begin to reexamine our definition of friendship.

Are the people with whom you surround yourself sharpening you or dulling you?

This isn't as clear-cut as this

It is nice to have someone with whom to go to Starbucks, to shop, or to talk with on the phone when you need a listening ear. However, biblical friendship runs deeper than that. Friendship needs to have as its foundation a desire to encourage each other's divinely appointed building project. Each one must continually make a purposeful effort to encourage and edify the other. Having coffee together can't be enough. You have to partner with people who challenge you spiritually and help you along in your building project, whatever it may be. Now, I am not implying that all of your conversations must be deep theological discussions and that you can never be silly and have fun. But we have to be careful who we allow into our close-knit circle of trusted friends. Believe it or not, those people influence the core of our lives. As parents, if we are concerned about the types of people our children befriend, is it not equally important for us to monitor friendships in the same manner?

If you are a single woman, this needs to be at the forefront of your mind as you consider potential candidates for marriage. The fact that a man is the most handsome man you've ever met is nice, but it is irrelevant. The amount of money in his portfolio is impressive, but it is hardly the most pertinent issue. Whether or not he has a bright future ahead on the horizon for his career does not matter most. What matters is whether this man has a hammer and a nail and is willing to get on his hands and knees to help you build! And are you willing to help him?

> *"Above all else, guard your heart, for it is the wellspring of life" (Proverbs 4:23).*

The people closest to you are helping to determine what type of "temple" you erect in your life and how quickly the building is completed. "Above all else, guard your heart, for it is the wellspring of life" (Proverbs 4:23). You and I must be diligent to protect our hearts and minds. Don't just practice this with members of the opposite sex but with all people in your sphere of influence. Take an inventory of who is feeding your spirit. Are they for or against your walking with the Lord? Remember, there is *no neutral ground*. Anyone who is not actively involved in helping you seek God and His will for your life is ultimately against what is most important to you.

Ask yourself the same questions about your friends that Zerubbabel asked in Ezra chapter four. "Does this person have anything in common with me for building? Are we equally yoked?" It is up to you to surround yourself with godly people who love you and have your best interests in mind, not only in the day-to-day physical realm but also in the eternal spiritual realm. Ask God to send people to you who will speak words of life to you and promote a healthy relationship between you and your Savior.

When I was young, my dad used to take our family to the circus. We would look across the arena when the lights went out and see all of these green, glow-in-the-dark plastic toys that people would tie around their wrists and necks. Of course, we wanted to be in on the action, so we would beg my father to buy one for each of us. Dad would spend $20 to get one for each of the four of us, and we had a blast with them while we were at the circus. The problem came when we got home and the glow faded.

Thankfully, my innovative father came up with a way to make it work again. He would turn on a lamp and tie those toys around the light bulb. Within a matter of minutes, they regained their glow. In fact, when you buy those toys, they are always hanging underneath a light source. This is because they don't just glow on their own; they gain their light from another source. After they are away from that source for a while, they lose their glow. In order to continue glowing day after day, they must charge up next to a greater light source.

You and I respond the same way. We need to be recharged! What type of people are you wrapping your life around? Are they sapping you of your energy, or are they helping you to retain and regain your glow? You and I need to be constantly wrapped around people in our church, our work, and our neighborhood who are helping infuse us with the power we need to glow for the glory of God. These are the people who are asking you what God's priorities are for your life and who want to help you get there. That is what friendship is really about! We need people who are going to help us, pray for us, and encourage us when life is not as we would like it to be. We need people who are going to turn our lives toward Christ Jesus.

Jada and I met when we were nine years old, and we have seen each other through every stage of life. Our birthdays are two weeks apart, our likes and dislikes are similar, and our educational, emotional, and spiritual lives have taken many of the same turns. Our friendship is fundamentally one spun out of our mutual love for God and our desire to serve Him. However, a friendship that begins at church or centers on Christian activities is not necessarily spiritually uplifting.

In a recent conversation, Jada stopped suddenly and asked, "So what is the Lord doing in your life?" This question startled me a bit since it had nothing to do with our previous discussion. This one question, however, turned the conversation away from us and onto the Lord. Although our friendship has always been a Christian relationship founded on God, Jada now makes it a point to intentionally ask questions and stir the discussion in a way that leaves each of us spiritually edified. She even recently invited me out for lunch for the express purpose of learning what God was doing in my life and how she might be praying for me. This must be a conscious effort in every relationship—a consistent resolve to edify, build up, and strengthen and encourage one another in faith (1 Thessalonians 3:2). Just being friends with a Christian does not guarantee that this will happen on its own; you must make a conscious decision and follow it through.

Pulling Together

One day a gentleman was on his way out of town, and his travels took him down a rural, dirt road. Somehow his car got knocked off of the road and into a ditch. A farmer who lived nearby saw the accident and rushed over to see if the gentleman was okay. The farmer asked, "Is there anything that I can do to help you?"

The man replied, "Yes, indeed. Do you have a horse or tractor that could help me pull my car out of this ditch so I can be on my way?"

The farmer thought for a while and then replied, "Well, sir, I do have a blind cow named Nellie." The man thought that this was odd, but he needed any help that he could get at this point.

The farmer went and got the blind cow named Nellie and hooked her up with all of the chains necessary to pull the car out of the ditch. The two men stood back, and the farmer yelled, "Cameron, pull!" Nothing happened. The farmer then yelled, "Sophie, pull!" and nothing happened. By this time, the man thought that the farmer must be nuts! The farmer yelled, "Casey, pull!" and still nothing happened. Then the farmer yelled, "Nellie, pull!" Immediately, the blind cow pulled with all of her might, and the car came right up out of that ditch.

The farmer unhooked the car and unshackled the cow, shook the man's hand, and was just about to leave. But the man stopped him and said, "I really appreciate your help, but I need to ask you a question. Why in the world did you call all of those other names before you called on Nellie to pull?"

The farmer said, "It's really simple. I told you that Nellie was a blind cow, right? If she had known that she was doing this all by herself, she never would have tried in the first place!"

If you are like me, you have at some point in your life felt exactly like that. We sometimes feel like we are pulling all by ourselves. You and I need to be encouraged by the knowledge that there are people to pull alongside us and help us when we fall into life's ditches. We need people who will help us pull when we get into financial ditches, emotional ditches, relational ditches, and the list goes on and on. Yet even with lots of friends around us, some of us feel like we are pulling all alone.

Sometimes we think we are okay with the quantity of friendships that we have without regard to their quality. Are all of the many people whom you call friends really doing what it takes to help you accomplish what the Lord is asking of you? Are *you* the type of friend that lines up with biblical guidelines? Are you pulling for your friends? Take inventory of your friendships, and pray that God will strip away those relationships that are not giving Him glory. Ask Him to send you sisters and brothers in Christ that will help turn your eyes toward the Lord and pull you in the right direction. Pray that God will guard you from this trap that prevented the children of Israel from reaching their goal of rebuilding the temple for many years. Don't let the company you keep take away from what God is doing in your life.

Don't let the company you keep take away from what God is doing in your life.

If your prayer is to become more like Jesus and to receive the benefits that we know our God can provide, then you can be sure that the Vinedresser will be coming into your life with pruning shears. You can be sure that the process of pruning will not be painless. However, the cutting away of external things like selfishness, misplaced security, and spiritually draining friendships indicates that He is at work inside you. Whether or not He prunes you and rids you of useless things will depend on what you do with the pain that you feel. Will you choose to rebel, or will you submit to the process and cooperate with the Master Gardener?

CHAPTER NINE

The Pitfall of
COMPARISON

AFTER THE ISRAELITES laid the foundation of the temple in Jerusalem under the leadership of Zerubbabel, they began to feel as though their work was insufficient. As we discovered earlier, they did not feel that they were capable of erecting a temple that would be as grand as Solomon's temple had been. Their discouragement was so paramount that many who had seen the former temple wept aloud when they saw the foundation of the new temple being laid (Ezra 3:12). The people knew that their available resources would not be adequate to do what they considered an adequate job of building. The Lord asked them through the prophet in Haggai 2:3, "Who of you is left who saw this house in its former glory? How does it look to you now? Does it not seem to you like nothing?"

The Jews were familiar with the prophetic messages of Isaiah, Jeremiah, and Ezekiel, which declared that, after the exiled people returned from Babylon, the reconstructed temple *would be* more splendid than the first temple their enemies had destroyed. The Old Testament writers raved about this first temple in detail in 2 Chronicles 2—4, a temple overlaid with the purest gold and adorned with precious stones. It had been constructed to include a pair of holy cherubim that were also overlaid with pure gold. The wingspan of the cherubim was enormous—so long, in fact, that one wing of each touched a side of the temple, and the two met in the middle. There was a "curtain of blue, purple and crimson yarn and fine linen, with cherubim worked into it" (2 Chronicles 3:14). Even the altar itself was made from bronze. God had dwelt there among His people by filling up this former, spectacular temple with His power and glory. From the perspective of the Jews in Ezra's time, duplicating this exquisite masterpiece was an impossible task. They knew that nothing they could build would compare, so they wanted to quit. And quit, they did. For about sixteen years, they laid the work of the Lord aside and went back to what they had been doing before they decided to put God's priorities ahead of their own. They were so concerned with what had been that they missed what they were currently supposed to be doing!

A New Work

The children of Israel spent a lot of time rehashing and bemoaning the past. Yet God is always doing a new thing! We compare our present existence with the way things used to be in "the good ol' days." Maybe we look back on the time before we had kids and think how easy life was then. Perhaps we reminisce about the days when we were single and wish we could go back and experience the freedom of being single again. Or maybe we remember our college and high school days and wish that we could live that carefree lifestyle all over again. We are often so concerned with the way things used to be that we miss the way things are supposed to be now. "Forget the former things; do not dwell on the past. See, I am doing a new thing! Now it springs up; do you not perceive it? I am making a way in the desert and streams in the wasteland" (Isaiah 43:18–19).

Often we are so wrapped up in yesterday and yesteryear that we don't experience His mercies for today.

Often we are so wrapped up in yesterday and yesteryear that we don't experience His mercies for today. We allow the lure of what used to be to keep us from experiencing the joy of what is to come. That is a trick of the devil. He wants to keep us looking backward. He knows that as long as we turn our attention in that direction, we will never move forward in our lives.

Remember, the Israelites longed for a good thing—a beautiful temple to worship God. We may even long for the fresh excitement and spiritual fervor we had when we first came to know the Lord. However, we shouldn't wish to change back into that former person. God wants to do a new thing—an even better thing. We should change into a new person—ever striving for new levels of faithfulness. "Because of the LORD's great love we are not consumed, for his compassions never fail. They are new every morning; great is your faithfulness" (Lamentations 3:22–23).

If you are driving down the road in your car, you can't do a good job of driving if your eyes focus steadily on the images in the rearview mirror. Yes, the rearview mirror is there for a good purpose, but you'd better not spend too much time looking in it or you'll get into big trouble! You are supposed to be looking forward and only checking the rearview mirror periodically in order to gain perspective. Likewise, you and I must spend our time looking forward to the changes God wants us to make now and not let what is in the rearview mirror of our lives consume us. To continue to look backward could cause a tragic and potentially fatal crash.

The Jews' building plans were thwarted because they were comparing what they were able to do with what someone else had done in the past. As human beings, we fall into this pattern far too easily. We say, "Lord, if I could just have her hair." "Lord, if I could just climb the ladder of success as fast as he is." "God, if I could just have a husband like that!" "Why is it that her children sit so still during the whole sermon? If my kids were like hers, my life would be so much easier!" We are always comparing ourselves to someone else, and we compare ourselves right out of the blessing that God has for us.

You Are Irreplaceable

There is absolutely no one like you on the face of the earth. In some translations, Genesis 2:22 says that God "fashioned" the woman. This term for "made" appears only once in the entire Creation story and implies that God took extra time and attention to detail when it came to His creation of woman. For everything else He created, the Bible says that God basically spoke, and "poof," there they were! (This might explain our problem with men!) Humans are not like all of the other works of His hands. He made us in His likeness and breathed into us His own breath. Then He went one step further and *fashioned* the woman uniquely and exquisitely. We ought to celebrate what He purposefully made us to be instead of spending our time wishing we were someone else. You are special. You are unique.

The personality, physical characteristics, gifts, talents, and abilities that God gave you are the "hammer and nails" that were strategically *fashioned by* God to complete the building project that He has assigned you. All you have to do is pick them up and get busy working. Your concern should not be the temple that someone else has constructed. You must focus your attention on the temple that He has asked you to build. Celebrate who you are, and get ready for God to do something great in your life! Quit wasting time wishing and hoping that your life would become like someone else's and that your building project will resemble theirs. God has you where you are for a purpose, and

He has created you with the equipment you need to live victoriously. Stop being consumed with the tools that *they have* . . . that's what *they* need for *their* construction. You have what you need. *Use it!*

When you become secure in who you are in Christ, you can then stop wasting time being jealous or envious of another. You don't have to wonder if someone else is better suited for that job you want or that man you would like to marry. You can stop being intimidated by another person, trying to avoid that person or, even worse, trying to bring that person down. If an encounter with God changes you, you can encourage others, celebrate who the Lord has made them to be, and trust in the Lord's ability to create you the way you need to be. There is so much freedom and peace in knowing who you are in Christ and knowing that He created you on purpose and with passion. When you recognize that He has given you the equipment you need for your building project, then you are free to celebrate the strengths of others! Each one of us has been divinely created with a unique purpose in mind and the tools necessary to fulfill that purpose.

We must ask the Lord to protect us from the desire to be something that we have not been created to be. Most of the time, we only know one side of the story of a person's life anyway. It becomes so easy for us to see the qualities in someone that we admire and want desperately to be like her when we don't know everything that would accompany our request. We never know what price someone has to pay for that trait that you covet so dearly.

Now don't get me wrong. There is nothing wrong with admiring someone's characteristics and godly traits and letting that serve as a catalyst for your own growth and change. That is very different from sulking in jealousy because another person has a fabulous singing voice and you don't.

Recognize that there is no one else like you and learn to accept yourself for what God has created in you; then you can appreciate the

Stop trying to be someone you are not.

strengths of others. Among the collage of people in this world, you are not a mistake. God didn't make you like your next-door neighbor or that woman at church or even your mother for a very good reason. It was no mistake! He did it on purpose. He has a plan mapped out, and He can use your personality, strengths, and weaknesses for His divine purposes. Stop trying to be someone you are not.

In a jigsaw puzzle, the pieces are all cut differently. The reason is simple: if they were all cut the same they wouldn't fit together. It is because of their different shapes that they are able to come together to make a beautiful picture. In the same way, you and I have to concentrate on how God made us and celebrate His originality in us. Rejoice over what God has done for you, and stop comparing yourself to other people. The children of Israel stopped their building project for the Lord because they were too busy making comparisons. They were distracted by what others had done and judged themselves by it. In doing so, they hindered the benefits the entire nation could have enjoyed.

When you and I refuse to accept God's unique design for our lives, it not only keeps us from reaching our full potential, but it also hinders the full progress of the entire body of Christ. Scripture makes clear that all the members of the body of Christ must work together. Paul says in 1 Corinthians 12:4–6, "There are different kinds of gifts, but the same Spirit. There are different kinds of service, but the same Lord. There are different kinds of working, but the same God works all of them in all men." God created you with your gifts, talents, and abilities for the common good of the body of Christ. What you bring to the table is necessary for all to succeed. And if you are busy trying to play someone else's role, who in the world is going to play yours? There is something that God has created you to do and accomplish. Get busy pursuing what He has for you, and it will become clear over time how you, in all your uniqueness, fit into the body of Christ. Paul continues in 1 Corinthians 12:14–18:

> *And if you are busy trying to play someone else's role, who in the world is going to play yours?*

good statement

> *Now the body is not made up of one part but of many. If the foot should say, "Because I am not a hand, I do not belong to the body," it would not for that reason cease to be part of the body. And if the ear should say, "Because I am not an eye, I do not belong to the body," it would not for that reason cease to be part of the body. If the whole body were an eye, where would the sense of hearing be? If the whole body were an ear, where would the sense of smell be? But in fact God has arranged the parts in the body, every one of them, just as he wanted them to be.*

God knew how you would complement the picture of His body, and He gifted you in the appropriate way. The problem? When most of us think of gifting, we are only able to see those people whose gifts bring them before an audience. We think of a gifted speaker, Bible teacher, or musician. We imagine being able to direct the choir on Sundays or lead praise and worship before the congregation. That seems like "real" ministry to us. Because those people are most often in the forefront, we esteem them more highly than we ought and forget the precious gifts of many who fade into the background.

Some of the most gifted people I know are those who serve faithfully in our church who aren't in the limelight at all. These people have the gift of serving, encouragement, and hospitality. These people are gifted to edify, intercede in prayer on behalf of others, and have faith in spite of terrible odds. These gifts are just as necessary. If we were all great preachers, then who would work in the children's ministry? If we all led praise and worship, then who would call out to God in intercession for the members? If we all taught the Bible in Sunday school, then who would be faithful to clean the church after the service and utilize gifts of service and hospitality? If we are all trying to move outside of our gifting, then we are not only stepping outside of the will of God for our lives, but we are also taking away from the full operation of the body of Christ.

No matter how insignificant you think your gifts or talents are, remember that none of them is insignificant to God.

No matter how insignificant you think your gifts or talents are, remember that none of them is insignificant to God. "Those parts of the body that seem to be weaker are indispensable, and the parts that we think are less honorable we treat with special honor" (1 Corinthians 12:22–23).

There is something to be said of those faithful servants of God who continue to pursue Him and serve Him when no one else is looking or cares to look. It is beautiful to meet someone whose heart is determined and focused on serving the Lord regardless of the spotlight being turned elsewhere.

My Aunt Elizabeth exemplifies this faithful kind of servanthood. At age forty-six, she is still single, yet without complaint. She finds her joy in serving the Lord faithfully in the areas in which she has been gifted. She has served as the director of our church's children's ministry for more than twenty-five years. Every Sunday and throughout the week, her car can be spotted in front of the sanctuary long before most have even gotten up in the morning. After the last car has departed from the parking lot after church, you can still see her car parked. As my mother's sister, she has been called "the sister-in-law of Dr. Tony Evans" for most of her life. She has stood beside my mother and encouraged my parents in the very visible ministry that God has called them to, yet she is comfortable with the fact that God has called her to a separate ministry that may not be to masses of people on radio and television but must still be done in faithful excellence.

Rarely does my aunt receive the spotlight of recognition. Rarely is she applauded for her years of service to children or to the other ministries in which she is involved, but she receives her satisfaction from knowing that God is well pleased with her faithful use of the gifts that He has given her. And now, decades after starting her service in the children's ministry, she is blessed to see the fruits of her labor as those children who grew up under her leadership in the church return as godly adults who are serving the Lord faithfully. Does she miss the recognition that she would receive if she served in a different arena? Not likely! She is recognized . . . by the fruits of her own hands.

You and I must also ask the Lord to show us where we are gifted and what He has called us to do. Then we must pursue Him wholeheartedly in that area. We must disregard the attention we may or may not receive, looking only toward the One on whom our eyes should focus.

Celebrating Our Differences

Making the decision to celebrate individual uniqueness has also been helpful in my marriage. It is freeing to finally come to a place where we appreciate our spouses and the little differences that make our relationship unique. I must admit that I am not the neatest person in the world. I keep a clean home, but I am not often concerned with the details and organization. While some women love to mop their floors, clean the

AND WE ARE CHANGED

windows, and organize drawers and closet space, I am the opposite. My home may look clean, but sometimes it is simply "straightened." In fact, cleaning my bedroom often means gathering up everything that is scattered on the floor and shoving it underneath the bed. I admit it!

This cleaning philosophy drives my husband nuts. He is a very detail-oriented person in every part of his life, including cleaning. I could clean all day long, and when my husband comes home, he could find something that I missed! This difference between us used to aggravate me, but I am slowly learning to appreciate it instead. Where I am weak, my husband is strong.

On the other hand, my husband could sit contentedly at home every weekend for the rest of his days without a social life. That type of existence sounds pretty close to death, if you ask me. I bring more spontaneity and fun into my husband's life. Where he is weak, I am strong. We both add something to the other's life that we would otherwise lack. Wouldn't all of our marriages run more smoothly if we would learn to appreciate our spouses' unique differences and celebrate those places where they are strong in our weakness? Try it in your marriage, and see what happens. Let this philosophy govern the way you view others and the gifts that they bring to your relationships.

> *This is what it means to be transformed—to have a consuming passion for the things of God.*

We must ask the Lord to show us our gifts and what He has called us to do and then pursue Him wholeheartedly in that area. This is what it means to be transformed—to have a consuming passion for the things of God.

When we have an encounter with God, it should change the way we look at other people and our own life situations. No longer should we be covetous of what others possess or what they have accomplished. We should not concentrate on their portion of the building project and let that distract us from being obedient to God in our own building assignment. We must gather the hammer and nails that the Lord has given us—our own abilities and talents—and focus on the "temple" that God has asked us to erect for His name's sake!   *Important*

The Miracle of

TRANSFORMATION

Ruth 1—4

CHAPTER TEN

A New IDENTITY

TUCKED IN THE MIDDLE of the Old Testament is a small, four-chapter book entitled Ruth—a short story of a dynamic girl from a foreign land. The book of Judges, which comes just before Ruth,

How often we turn away from following Him, even though He is consistently merciful and kind to us.

describes a turbulent time in Israel's history. The last line of Judges attests to the chaos of the time: "In those days Israel had no king; everyone did as he saw fit" (Judges 21:25). Translation? At the time of Ruth and the judges, Israel was rebelling against God and living in sin. Rape, murder, homosexuality, faithlessness, and spiritual and moral depravity permeated the land. Even so, God called the people of Israel to Himself, despite their repeated offenses. Despite the fact that throughout the Old Testament they left their merciful God and served other gods. Despite the fact that those rescued from Egypt continued to rebel as if He had done nothing for them. Despite their persistent disregard for the love of their heavenly Father. Despite all of this, God still loved them and continued to call the rebellious children of Israel to Himself. Isn't this the picture of God's relationship with us? How often we turn away from following Him, even though He is consistently merciful and kind to us.

If we look back to the beginning of the book of Ruth, we see Ruth as she was before her encounter with God. Her story begins with a Jewish man named Elimelech, his wife Naomi, and their two sons, Mahlon and Kilion. Because Israel had been disobedient, there was a severe famine in the land, so Elimelech moved his family from their hometown of Bethlehem to Moab, where the food was plentiful. However, in Moab they met with disaster. Elimelech died, and Naomi "was left with her two sons" (Ruth 1:3). Then the two sons married Moabite women, Orpah and Ruth.

The touching story of Ruth is placed in the middle of this tumultuous conflict between a loving God and His rebellious children. If I did not believe in the divine inspiration of the Bible, I might be inclined to think that the book of Ruth was misplaced. But of course, there is no mistake here. In fact, the book's placement is quite deliberate. Ruth is purposely juxtaposed with Judges to show us the contrast between true godliness and utter chaos. The message of this young woman's life provides hope and encouragement during a desperate period. Ruth's story demonstrates how God uses someone who has committed to change as a result of an encounter with Him. In contrast to Israel, who encountered God and continued to rebel, Ruth encountered God and was transformed—forever! God not only used her to touch her family, her community, and her nation but also the entire world through her place in the messianic line! As we see so clearly in Ruth's life, an encounter with God should change the way we function in a disobedient and dying world. When all around us is dark, we have been called to be the light!

Although Ruth's life ultimately has a happy ending, she was well acquainted with tragedy. She encountered the unexpected deaths of loved ones, the pain of difficult decisions, and other trials. This is a reminder to us that our encounters with God do not shield us from trouble; they simply equip us to handle personal trials in a radically different way. Jesus clearly warns us that we will have trouble in this world (John 16:33). Just because we know and love Him does not mean we are exempt from life's hardships. However, if you have had an encounter with God, then you can rest assured that the same God who acted on your behalf yesterday is the same God who will act on your behalf today and tomorrow and forever.

Even in the midst of Israel's desperation as a whole and Ruth's personal trials in particular, God was weaving a web of events that would cause her to be the catalyst of a miracle. She simply had to yield to His will and obey His promptings. When she did, her life and the lives of others she touched were changed . . . completely.

Light in the Darkness

Since the backdrop of the book is so dark, God positioned Ruth in such a way to show the great disparity between light and darkness. In contrast to a dark nation, this woman's life and faith shone brightly. As Christians, God has likewise called us to be the light in the darkness. He has strategically placed us to shine for Him and to guide others to the light of His truth.

Light has many purposes, but perhaps its chief purpose is to illumine the path. Light is a beacon in the midst of darkness, showing the way and penetrating even the darkest places where our vision fails us. Light is a life-giving, life-saving force in our world, as this story I heard shows.

One dark night a ship sailed out at sea. The captain navigated their course by using the powerful light on the ship. As they traveled across the still water, the captain spotted another headlight coming in his direction. One of these vessels was going to have to move out of the other's path to avoid sure calamity. Over the ship's loudspeaker the captain announced with authority, "Move 30 degrees north."

A voice floated back across the water toward him, "No, you move 30 degrees south."

Once again, the captain urged, "Please move 30 degrees north."

Again, the other voice responded, "You move 30 degrees south."

By this time the captain was growing both frustrated and a little nervous. The giant light was coming nearer and nearer, and they were in great danger. The captain declared emphatically, "I am a captain in the United States Navy, and I demand that you immediately move 30 degrees to the north."

A voice came back and said, "You move 30 degrees south. I am the lighthouse!"

When you are the lighthouse, you are the one calling the shots! My friend, you are the spiritual lighthouse in a dark world. As the spiritual light for your home, your workplace, or your community, you don't move! Everyone else must shift their positions around you. You are to take your place in the midst of the darkness of your circumstances and stand firm. As the lighthouse, you must set the course rather than be set by it.

> *Many believers are so busy trying to fit in with the world that we are not setting the standard anymore.*

Unfortunately, many believers are so busy trying to fit in with the world that we are not setting the standard anymore. We are adapting too much to how the world says we should live. It should be the other way around—we should be changing the world rather than the world changing us. We have seen this to be true in our individual lives and collectively as the church. On the

140

whole, we as the corporate body of Christ have been too quiet. The light of Christians is sadly dim on issues such as reinstating prayer in schools, abortion laws, and political reform. We speak ill of the graphic scenes on our television and movie screens, yet we contribute to the robust bottom line on opening night. Sadly, our lives are often not distinguishable from the lives of others around us.

God is light (1 John 1:5), and He has called His people to shine His light into a dark world. Our walk, not just our talk, should illuminate the truth that the loving, powerful God still sits on the throne of heaven, and He is the ruler of all people in all circumstances. Are we shining brightly, or have we dimmed and faded into the background?

"You are the light of the world. A city on a hill cannot be hidden. Neither do people light a lamp and put it under a bowl. Instead they put it on its stand, and it gives light to everyone in the house. In the same way, let your light shine before men, that they may see your good deeds and praise your Father in heaven" (Matthew 5:14–16).

When we shine the light of Christ in our lives, we will find that the world is strangely attracted to the light.

If three hundred people were in a dark room without any light, the result would be utter chaos. Yet if one person had a flashlight, the others would be attracted to that source of light to illumine the way to safety. When we shine the light of Christ in our lives, we will find that the world is strangely attracted to the light. They are curious, interested, even compelled to come. Deep inside they sense that the true Light is their only hope of safety in this dark world, and we have that truth! If we simply shine brightly our light for Christ Jesus, we will no longer have to plead with our neighbors or co-workers to come to our church services. We simply have to illume the pathway to God. When people see the true God in our lives, they will come.

Strategically Placed

Ruth's encounter with God began long before she was aware of it. Before the book of Ruth opens, the invisible hand of a loving, holy, sovereign God was already moving to secure her place in a tumultuous time in history. How could she have guessed that she would play an important part in God's will?

In the same way, we often cannot see Him as clearly as we would like, but His work in us has already begun. "He who began a good work in you will carry it on to completion until the day of Christ Jesus" (Philippians 1:6). The truth is reflected in the words of a song I've heard: "When you can't trace His hand, trust His heart." I love that! Every moment of your life He is working to orchestrate events in order to accomplish His will in your life. When you are in His will, He can use you to influence others. Whether or not you can see Him or feel His presence is irrelevant. You must trust that He is there and that He is at work to create a place for you to shine.

Perhaps you think that the world is so huge that you cannot make a difference in it. It seems that you can barely make any strides in your own situation, much less in the community or the world. I'm sure Ruth felt the same way. But God was positioning her to make a difference in her sphere of influence. Consider now the different spheres of influence in which the Lord has placed you, including those places where it may be hard for you to grasp what God is doing: a stressful, secular work environment, a monotonous carpool to the kids' school, or a boring commute on the train to work. Remember that God has strategically placed you in the midst of your circumstances as His little lighthouse. He planned and orchestrated it. It is not by mistake that you are there.

Are you shining right where you are? If you are unappreciated or teased by your peers or co-workers for doing what is right, then you are shining for Christ! If you are ridiculed by others for your ideas and opinions or talked about by your single friends because of the lifestyle you choose, so be it. If you are lonely because of your stand for God, He knows where you are, and He will meet you. God has placed you where you are. Do not quit your job because everyone is so ungodly. That's why you are there! You are His strategically placed light. Do not move out of that neighborhood. You are His representative. Do not leave your unsaved family behind. You are the one who will illuminate the way to safety.

He has strategically placed you to interrupt the darkness of your circumstances and the circumstances of those around you. In fact, you and I can truly know that we are serving Christ wholeheartedly and being witnesses for Him when others do reject and persecute us.

> *Dear friends, do not be surprised at the painful trial you are suffering, as though something strange were happening to you. But rejoice that you participate in the sufferings of Christ, so that you may be overjoyed when his glory is revealed. If you are insulted because of the name of Christ, you are blessed, for the Spirit of glory and of God rests on you.*
>
> *1 Peter 4:12–14*

In this passage, Peter goes on to say that no believer should suffer for doing evil, but if any of us suffer for being Christians, we should glorify God. This leads us to a reasonable conclusion: If everybody likes you and if no one ever questions your ideals and belief system, then you should examine whether or not you are truly serving God wholeheartedly.

When we truly serve the Lord and live as He desires, we cannot expect the world to applaud. People on your job, in your neighborhood, and in your school should perceive you as a little strange. Don't be discouraged if you find yourself without friends or with direct enemies because of your service to the Lord. You should expect it. You aren't like them. In fact, it is a great tragedy if you do resemble them. You cannot serve Christ the way you should and have a lifestyle that is identical to all of your ungodly friends. That would be impossible. How can your heavenly Father be the Father of Light and another person's father be the Prince of Darkness, yet the two of you appear to be twins? What about the change?

The word "holy" means to be set apart. You have been called to a life of holiness. It is time for you to draw a line in the sand, set your standards, and make a decision to be holy. We have been chosen by God to live a life that looks different from the world. Get rid of anything that does not foster a holy lifestyle, and try to display the brightest light possible to the world. In case you have not noticed, our world needs to see light now like never before, and we must be bold in the declaration of our faith.

When I was in college, darkness surrounded me. My neighbors during my first year were atheists. I had known non-Christians, but up until that point I had never really befriended anyone who firmly believed there was no God. I called my dad right away and asked many questions about their belief system. Often these young men living down the hall would specifically say or do things to repulse my roommate and me. They would intentionally use the Lord's name in vain, curse, and use other lewd language that they knew my roommate and I would find repulsive.

Yet I continued to do my best to share my faith when I could. Although I certainly was not perfect during college, one thing I was serious about was telling people about Jesus. I can recall going around campus with a friend of mine telling anyone who would listen that Jesus was the answer. People thought I was crazy. I eventually graduated from college and closed that chapter of my life.

About a year ago, a young man walked up to me while I was attending a banquet for Dallas Theological Seminary. He looked somewhat familiar, but I didn't remember who he was. He smiled broadly and introduced himself. As he talked, he began to look more familiar to me. He was one of the young men in college who had laughed at me when I had tried to share Jesus with him! Without my saying a word, he brought up his behavior in college and immediately apologized. I couldn't believe my ears!

Before I could even respond, he went on to explain that because of what I had done, he had received Jesus and was now attending seminary. I was simply amazed at God's work. I was so excited that in some small way and despite my own shortcomings God had used me as an instrument in this man's salvation.

The Lord is now using this young man in incredible ways to minister internationally. That day the Lord reminded me that He will reward those who suffer for Him . . . even if it takes longer than we might hope. I never imagined that my steadfast efforts at evangelism at the University of Houston would have international repercussions. If you find yourself in similar circumstances, do not be dismayed because of those who mistreat you for your faith. God will use you, and the joy you will feel when the reward comes will be beyond what you can imagine.

Perfectly Prepared

"But I don't know if I have what it takes to be a light on my job. You haven't seen how dark that place is." Ever thought that? Ruth may have had similar sentiments when she entered the Israelite culture during one of its darkest periods. God transplanted this young woman from her home and culture into Israel, into a world totally outside her comfort zone. She also must have felt ill equipped and unable. However, God knew that Ruth was up for the task ahead. From the day of her birth, He had prepared her to do His will later in her life. He had equipped her with the character, personality, and appearance necessary for His purposes. Despite her personal faults and faulty circumstances, He used her. He chose her to be an example to us of what light looks like when our whole world is very dark.

In His wisdom, God has not only chosen you for your specific position; He has also prepared you for it. He is not shocked or surprised by the darkness that you find all around you. It is by His design so that you, His lighthouse, can shine for His glory. You are perfectly prepared. Before you were even born, the Lord knew what He had in store for your life, and He made sure that you had everything you would need to be a bright light for His kingdom here on earth.

> *Your encounter with God is in progress right now! It has already begun!*

Do you see? Your encounter with God is in progress right now! It has already begun! We must never think for a moment that our station in this life fell upon us simply by chance or default. It is God's divine plan. You are not where you are by mistake, nor are you the way you are by accident. The Holy God of the universe gave you your personality, characteristics, physical appearance, and other unique gifts because He knew what your life would entail and what you would need to shine His light to the world.

When I was pregnant with our son, everything about my body changed. All of a sudden my favorite sleeping position no longer felt comfortable. My favorite clothes no longer fit quite right or for that matter . . . at all! Some of my favorite exercises were banned by my doctor. And a lot of my favorite foods (namely bacon cheeseburgers) no longer agreed with my stomach. This new life altered every aspect of my body. I was not in control anymore; that little baby was running the show! I ate when he said it was time to eat and only what he liked. No matter how much stuff there was to do around the house, I took a nap when he said it was time to rest. No matter what clothes I desired to wear, his ever-growing body determined my shape and thus my wardrobe. I was completely under the control of the new life inside of me.

When you became a Christian, a new life set up residence in you. You now have the life of Jesus Christ inside, and that should change you completely, from the inside out. Your sleeping arrangements should change. Your eating habits should change. The clothes you choose to wear should be different, and your work and play schedules should change. Why? Because you are under the control of the One inside of you, the One who is in charge now.

Now that you have encountered the God of the universe and He has infiltrated your existence, your identity has drastically altered. Everything about you should be different.

Nobody into Somebody

There is something very crucial that you must know about Ruth. She wasn't a citizen of Israel; she was a Moabitess. God used someone who was not one of His "chosen" people. In the eyes of the Jews, she was a lesser human, a barbaric pagan. She wasn't trained in the Jewish law, religion, and culture. She didn't worship or even know the one true God. She didn't fit the profile of someone that we would expect God to use. She was like many of us—born on the wrong side of the tracks and seemingly headed nowhere. Like her, we may feel rejected because of our backgrounds. Our history and education may seem unacceptable, and others may look upon us with disdain. Our appearance and possessions may be inferior in others' eyes. We may not know the spiritual lingo or possess the high-profile spiritual gifts. Many of us may feel more like Ruth than the chosen children of Israel.

Ruth was not of the chosen nation, yet she was the one God called to serve as an example of righteousness in the Old Testament. Because she was qualified? Because she was an outstanding religious person? Because she was especially gifted and talented? She was none of these things, but she was willing! I have good news. You don't have to be qualified for God to use you. God uses those of us who are simply willing to obey. Ruth's life reminds us that it does not matter what you look like or where you do and don't fit in. It doesn't even matter how your past looks. What matters is the change.

In fact, the Lord loves to choose the least likely people. He most often uses the misfits, those who, to human eyes, have obvious signs of weakness in their lives. Why? In our weakness, His strength is perfect. It is when we are at our weakest point that His glory and power are most evident.

> *God doesn't call the equipped; He equips the called!*

You may think that you are ill equipped, but that is irrelevant. We are all ill equipped! He doesn't need *our* equipment to take care of *His* business! We need His equipment, and the Bible declares emphatically that He has "given us everything we need for life and godliness" (2 Peter 1:3). All we need is Him and what He has to give. God doesn't call the equipped; He equips the called!

When you have an encounter with God, as Ruth did, it changes your identity. It changes who you are from the inside out. It overrides anything that you think disqualifies you from being used by God. In fact, if those who *seem*, in earthly terms, to be most useful to God are unwilling to obey, He will use someone else.

This is the picture we have in the story of Ruth. The children of Israel were not willing to do what He asked them to do, so He brought in an outsider who was. God's ultimate goal is always that His righteous, perfect will be accomplished on this earth. With or without you, He will get it done. The question is whether or not you will obey and join Him in the process. I don't know about you, but I want to be right smack-dab in the middle of God's will for my life. I want to be a part of the story that God is telling in this generation. Ruth was the one chosen to be the lighthouse to her generation—to stand in the midst of the darkness that the "chosen ones" had created. She is the one who served the Lord. At that point her past and her lack of credentials became irrelevant!

New Identity

When Naomi and Elimelech moved to Moab, their sons married Moabite women, Orpah and Ruth. However, God had instructed Jewish men not to take wives from foreign cultures, specifically from Moab (Deuteronomy 23:3). God's purpose was simply to protect the purity of the Jewish religion and the Jews' special relationship with God by keeping false gods, idols, and foreign religious practices from infiltrating their culture. If a man's wife brought pagan practices into the marriage, she brought along temptation. The man, because of his sinful heart, might allow or even participate in the practices.

However, Ruth's heart, under the influence of Naomi, her godly mother-in-law, began to turn toward the God of Israel. I can imagine that Naomi, whose name meant "amiable and pleasant," probably sought to bridge the gap between herself and her new daughters by telling them about the awesome God she served. I can picture the young women seated at her feet as she told them about Moses, the Red Sea, the Promised Land, and the great wonders that her people had experienced. Ruth and Orpah probably became very interested in their new family's world. I am certain that Ruth's identity changed because of her marriage into this family. Due to her marriage, she learned more about the God of Israel, and God began to transform who she was.

At that time in Jewish culture, marriage meant more than just taking on the family name. Marriage also meant assuming the family

149

identity. The wife's identity was to become one with her new husband's. Ruth's and Orpah's decisions to marry into this Jewish family probably should have affected every aspect of their emotional, physical, and spiritual lives.

Although there were some scriptural exceptions to this rule, when a young woman married into a particular family, she was expected to take on that family's religious beliefs. She became a part of the very fabric of her husband's family. She did not hyphenate her name and hold on to pieces of her past. She became all that her husband's family was. Her identity was progressively changed. Ruth's decision to marry this man extended beyond her commitment just to him. She was now committed to this family. So that even if her husband died, she was still bound to her new family. There was no running back to Mom and Dad. She had a new name, a new family, and a brand-new identity.

God's desire for us is that we recognize that we are a part of His family now. He doesn't want the "new" you to have a hyphenated name with the "old" you waiting in the wings. God wants your identity to be changed without reservation. He wants us to understand that since we said yes to Christ's proposal of holy matrimony, we are wedded to Him and are a part of His family. Our progressive sanctification throughout life is the process by which we become more like Christ and less like our old selves. Our commitment to this process must be unshakeable, no matter what circumstances we face. There can be no running back to our former lifestyles. We must be fully committed with all of our hearts. He longs for an unbridled love relationship with us.

This is the kind of love that Ruth seemed to have for her new family. She had been raised to love her family in Moab, their way of doing things, and the gods that their community served. She left all that she knew to commit her life to a man who won her heart. The Lord wants to win our hearts away from our former affections and transform us into His radiant bride. An encounter with our Bridegroom will certainly call us away from who we once were and change our identity.

CHAPTER ELEVEN

A Changed
PATH

RUTH'S ENCOUNTER with God did not protect her from tragedy; it prepared her to make the right decisions once tragedy came her way. And she didn't have to wait long for it to arrive. Not only did Ruth's father-in-law die, but after just ten years of marriage, her husband died as well. Ruth was a young, childless widow in a pagan culture and surrounded by grief.

What darkness has hit home with you recently? Has your company decided to lay you off? Were you having a hard enough time being thirty and still single, and now all of your friends are getting married and asking you to be the maid of honor? Have you lost a friend or a loved one too soon? Are you having a hard time conceiving a child, and now your sister or best friend is pregnant with a healthy baby? What is it that has hit home with you?

Don't be dismayed. When the darkness hits close to home in your life, you'd better get ready, because, just like Ruth, you are in for a big move of God!

When life gets painful, don't hang your head in despair. Look up. Keep your eyes open for the next move of God. He is preparing you for something big. Your heavenly Father's next move is . . .

more radical than your terrifying crisis

more stunning than your devastating pain

more powerful than your overwhelming circumstances

more miraculous than your wildest imagination.

God's next move is *awesome*, and He is preparing you to receive it. You must now position yourself to change paths.

On September 15, 1999, Wedgewood Baptist Church in Ft. Worth, Texas, made national news when an armed gunman made his way into a service and opened fire. The church lost seven members, and several others were injured. The media drew attention to this Baptist church as it went through a season of darkness. All eyes turned to this hurting body of believers. When the press interviewed Al Meredith, the pastor of the church, they asked how the church was going to be able to cope in the face of such tragic circumstances. In a bold voice, the minister proclaimed that when believers face difficulties and trials of this nature, our task is not to spend our time looking at the circumstances but rather to look up—to turn our attention to the Lord. How powerful this statement proved to be as the entire nation watched this church survive and thrive through God's grace.

Position yourself for a change by looking up!

Whatever darkness looms in your life, don't stare at the heartache and the hurt. Position yourself for change by looking up! God is trying to show you some-thing, and His desire is to turn your attention to Him. You must be correctly positioned, focusing upward, in order to see the good hand of God working on your behalf.

So "look not only to your own interests" (Philippians 2:4) but rather . . .

Look toward the hills, where your help comes from (Psalm 121:1).

Seek the Lord while He may be found (Isaiah 55:6).

Come to Jesus (Matthew 14:29).

Behold the Lamb of God (John 1:29).

Look ahead to the reward (Hebrews 11:26).

Seek Him and His face (Psalm 24:6).

Search for Him with all your heart (Psalm 119:2).

Long for a better place (Hebrews 11:16).

Set your heart on things above (Colossians 3:1).

Scripture promises in Deuteronomy 4:29 that if "you seek the LORD your God, you will find him if you look for him with all your heart and with all your soul." So don't waste time and energy looking every-where else! Just look up before you take your next step! He will direct your path.

Making Wise Choices

After Ruth lost her husband, she had to decide which path to take next. Often our reaction to personal pain will cause us to move in a different direction. Unfortunately, that path will often be one that takes us outside of the will of God. We will find ourselves so disillusioned by the discomfort in our lives that we will make knee-jerk decisions that hurt us in the end. We need to make sure that in these times when we feel most vulnerable, we are carefully making wise choices. We must look upward to see what the Lord would have us do and what He is trying to teach us so that we can make the right decision.

What I love about Ruth is not what we read about her after the death of her husband—it's what we *don't* read. We are not told that she was so overtaken by her loss that her emotional distress became totally consuming. We know that the Bible records emotion. An entire book of the Bible is called Lamentations, which means "to lament or cry." We know that David danced and cried before the Lord in the book of Psalms. We know that even Jesus wept, suffered, and experienced pain. In Ruth's story, Naomi's emotion and overwhelming feelings of bitterness over the loss of her husband and two sons are recorded. Undoubtedly Ruth was saddened by the loss of her husband, yet she did not allow her sadness to cripple her for the rest of her life. She chose to overcome it and pursue a new direction in life. What an incredible lesson is tucked away here in what we do not read about Ruth!

When you and I are saddened by life's trials, it is acceptable to be sad, upset, and even angry, but it is not acceptable to allow these emotions to overtake and control us. This is precisely what the devil wants. You do not have to be consumed with bitterness, fear, sadness, or depression. No matter how devastating your circumstances are, you have the spiritual right as a child of God to be free from the emotional scars that accompany life's pain. You may never be free from the memory of what caused your pain, but you can be free from the emotional trauma that resulted from it. The Bible declares you to be an overcomer by the blood of the Lamb (Revelation 12:11). Because of your encounter with the Lord, you do not have to be overcome or overwhelmed by the circumstances of life. You can choose a different emotional path. You have a choice to either be enslaved to the emotions that accompany life's pains or to be free.

During this time of emotional distress after the death of her husband and two sons, Naomi decided that the best thing for her was to return to Bethlehem. She knew that it would be hard for her and her two daughters-in-law to survive in Moab alone. Plus, she had heard "that the LORD had come to the aid of his people by providing food for them" (Ruth 1:6), so there was no reason to stay away from Bethlehem any longer. Moab had become a place of sadness and loneliness for Naomi, and she longed to be in her homeland.

Right in the middle of their life-altering decision to choose a new path, they had a chance to turn back.

The two young women would have faithfully followed their mother-in-law wherever she went. They were committed to this Israelite family and all that it represented, so all three women "set out on the road that would take them back to the land of Judah" (Ruth 1:7). Don't miss this particular line in the story. They were on their way—bags packed and minds made up—when something happened. Right in the middle of their life-altering decision to choose a new path, they had a chance to turn back. Naomi turned to them in the midst of the journey, released them from their commitment to her, and gave them the option of returning to Moab.

Have you ever noticed how the enemy waits until we are at our deepest places of hurt to tempt us? He knows us very well, and he knows how to take our eyes off the right path. Often Satan will use our emotional pain during times like these to steer us in the wrong direction.

Moab would have been a more logical choice for both of these women. It was where they had grown up and where they had established their whole lives. In their hearts, they would have longed to go back to where they had always called home. Most of us would have chosen Moab if given the same option.

I was born and raised in Dallas and have lived there most of my life. I only lived four hours away for undergraduate studies and returned to get my Master's degree in Dallas. I do a lot of traveling, but I must say that there is no place like Dallas anywhere on the face of the earth! It is home to me in every sense of the word. It is the place where I feel comfortable, where I have friends, where my family lives, and where I know how to get around. I can only imagine how hard it would be if for some reason Jerry told me we needed to move away from Dallas. I would struggle so much with that decision, because this is all I have known my entire life.

I suppose this must have been how Ruth and Orpah felt as well. They knew the ins and outs of their home city, and their family and friends were there. Moab was their home. Naomi's offer to allow them to return home silently appealed to all of these things.

However, when you and I have an encounter with God it changes the paths we choose—regardless of our comfort zones. It changes the course we would normally have charted for our lives. It directs our attention away from those things that are pleasing in our eyes and onto those things that are pleasing in His! No matter how inviting the "Moab" of your old life may look, determine to choose a different path that will lead you according to God's plans for you. You are almost there! Don't turn back.

Leaving Comfort Behind

Perhaps the thing that endears me to Dallas the most is that my parents' home is there. The most comfortable and soothing place in the whole world is my mom's house! Even though I have my own house now, which has begun to feel like home to me, there will probably never be a place that offers me the peaceful, happy feeling that I get in the home where I grew up. Many of us women still feel that the safest, most comfortable place in the world is back in Mom's warm, inviting nest.

Naomi zeroed in on this feeling when she said to the girls, "Go back, each of you, *to your mother's home*" (Ruth 1:8) (italics mine). Deep down, all of us want to feel comfortable. We pay high prices for conveniences that bring comfort to our lives. Naomi realized that the Jewish people would have a hard time warming up to these pagan women. Ruth and Orpah were used to being welcomed in their mamas' houses. The Jews would likely treat them as foreigners and even potential enemies. Yet in order for Ruth and Orpah to choose God's path for them, they had to leave Moab and the warm welcome at Mama's house. They had to leave comfort behind.

In order to experience the new things that God has in store for us, we have to be willing to step out of our comfort zones. We must come to a place in our lives where we accept that physical and even emotional comforts are not priorities. In fact, I believe that the reason many Christians do not see more supernatural power at work in their lives is because they refuse to leave their comfort zones. If we always operate in our areas of knowledge and skill, or if we only do things in which we excel, we will never leave room for the Almighty God to move in our midst. Scripture says that He demonstrates His strength when we are weak (2 Corinthians 12:9). He doesn't show up when we are operating in comfort. He shows up when we are weaklings—nervous and in need of Him. I once heard this memorable statement: "If you do what you have always done, you will get what you have always gotten!" I don't want

> *If you do what you have always done, you will get what you have always gotten!*

what I have always gotten; I want a miracle from God. When we move outside of those areas that are second nature to us, we give the Lord room to move in supernatural ways to fulfill our needs and in some cases our desires.

What is your comfort zone? Obviously the answer to that question is going to be different for each of us, depending on our personal strengths, talents, and experiences. Our comfort zone is the place where we can function confidently on our own, without recognizing our desperate need for the Holy Spirit's help. For me, this principle of stepping outside my comfort zone and giving God room to work holds true when I am addressing an audience. My first inclination is to pick out a familiar text of Scripture to teach. However, I have often felt the Holy Spirit moving me in a different direction, sometimes at the last minute! He has prompted me to teach on something that I do not feel adequately prepared to deliver. I wish I could say that I have always followed His leading, but I haven't, and the consequence was a presentation that, although well prepared, did not bring conviction to the hearts of the listeners. In contrast, I have discovered that on the occasions when I was obedient to the leading of the Holy Spirit, God moved in an incredible way. The text of Scripture became alive to me and to all who were in attendance. That happened not because of what I was prepared to do but because of what *He was* prepared to do. All I had to do was get out of the way so that He could work supernaturally.

I am confident that when Christians move away from our comfortable nests and tap into new areas, we will experience God's power. Christians can no longer tuck themselves quietly away inside the familiar walls of the church. Now is the time for us to come out of the sanctuary and flood the streets for Jesus! We need to be where the prostitutes and drug addicts are. We need to go to the inner city where families are decaying, to be light where light is most needed. Unfortunately, churches have become a haven for the well dressed, well educated, and well positioned. We are too comfortable. We sit in our comfortable pews with our expensive clothes and finely-bound leather Bibles. But Jesus said, "It is not the healthy who need a doctor, but the sick" (Mark 2:17). As God's children, we must leave our cozy corners and step out boldly into the blistering cold of the world. It is time for the comfort of Moab to be left behind in my life and in yours so that we can continue on the way to the land of Judah. What place of comfort is the Lord requesting that you leave behind:

that comfortable relationship

that comfortable habit

that comfortable career

that comfortable guilt

that comfortable isolation

that comfortable addiction?

The list goes on and on. What is it for you?

Comfort is one convenience that most of us are not willing to give up. We want to have everything when and how we want it, and we have a bitter attitude if we don't get it that way. I have had to check myself on many occasions (and still do) to remind myself that my comfort should not be my main goal; His glory should be my priority.

Leaving Your Desires Behind

Naomi gives her second plea to the girls in Ruth 1:9. "May the LORD grant that each of you will find rest in the home of another husband." Naomi indicates to them that if they want to marry again, then their best bet would be to stay in Moab.

Ruth and Orpah were probably very young women. If they had married when they were young teenagers, they were already widows in their early twenties. Although they would have been considered "older

women" in their times, they likely would have married again. Ruth and
Orpah probably longed to remarry and to have the love, security, and
protection of a husband. Yet by leaving Moab, the likelihood of remar-
rying was slim to none. The Jewish people held a disdain for them, and
the young Jewish men would probably not choose an older bride from a
foreign land. To leave Moab was to leave behind one of the deepest
longings of their hearts and face a life of being an unmarried widow.

When we are ready to make a change, it may require that we be
willing to leave behind some of the things that we want the most in our
lives. Being transformed means that no matter what we desire, we are
still willing to press toward what God wants for us because of our
commitment to Him.

That desire you have to conceive a child will have to be left
behind in Moab. The desire to find a mate will have to be left behind.
The longing to achieve success in your career, to be noticed or
applauded, or to build that ministry exactly the way you want it—these
will have to go. Now, in His great mercy to us, He may choose to grant
us some of these things, but in order to move
expeditiously to Judah, you and I cannot be
burdened with the expectations we have for
our lives. The journey to our new lives in
Judah is on foot, led by the Spirit. That means
no extra baggage. This is no cozy airline
flight—you don't get a carry-on! When God
calls us away from Moab, we must willingly
leave behind all of our goals, ambitions, aspi-
rations, and longings in anticipation of what
He has in Judah. Are you willing?

Your willingness to leave your desires behind shows the Lord your commit-ment to Him.

The Lord may give you what you desire,
but your willingness to leave your desires
behind shows the Lord your commitment to
Him and leaves room for Him to operate with-

out interruption. Now this gets very tricky for us, doesn't it? It is so easy to say that we are willing to leave behind those things that are important to us. But are we really?

For example, in order to figuratively press toward the land of Judah, the probability of a single woman's getting married might dwindle. Statistics tell us that for every seven available African-American women, there is one black available male. All that means is that he is of the same African descent and that he is not married. It does not mean that he is growing spiritually, loves the Lord, has a desire to please Him, or even has a job, for that matter! It just means he is available. I know you want more than that! If you want someone who is in love with God (I don't mean to make you nervous), the statistic jumps from 7:1 to 25:1! Those statistics are fairly similar regardless of your ethnicity. That is enough to make you cry, isn't it? It would be . . . if you didn't know that the Lord had everything under control and that "he rewards those who earnestly seek him" (Hebrews 11:6).

> *The beauty of our God's gift-giving is that He doesn't give us what we want but what we need.*

Psalm 27:13 says, "I am still confident of this: I will see the goodness of the LORD in the land of the living." God didn't check the statistics before He made the plans for your life! He was not concerned with ratios or probabilities. He just wants to know if you are willing to obey, even if it costs you. Don't despair, for when God sees that you willingly leave behind your most important desire for His sake, He will reward you immensely. He may not necessarily answer in the way you expect, but He will answer in a way that supersedes your initial request in the first place!

In fact, what kind of God would He be if all He could offer us was what we asked of Him? The beauty of our God's gift-giving is that He doesn't give us what we want but what we need. He can see past the words that we pray, beyond the tears that we cry, and straight to the bottom line of our lives. He can see what is best for us and what we need even (and especially) when we cannot.

Leaving Conformity Behind

Naomi's pleas apparently proved to be too much for Orpah to resist, and she finally turned back to her homeland. Ruth was the only one left when Naomi gave her third and final plea. "Your sister-in-law is going back to her people and her gods. Go back with her" (Ruth 1:15). Naomi suggested that since Orpah had chosen to go, Ruth should also.

In our lives, Moab represents the place where "everybody else is doing it." Moab welcomes you to be a part of the crowd. It is where you will easily fade into your environment. You will conform to your surroundings in Moab, because you will be so similar to those with whom you work, play, and live. Ruth's latest temptation was that her sister-in-law had gone back to her old way of life; should she follow suit?

Let's be honest with ourselves. We find a certain level of comfort in being like everybody else. We like the feeling of being part of the "in" crowd, even if that means sacrificing what God would have us do.

I was a very successful student in high school. I made good grades, was a cheerleader, and ran on the track team. I was always voted "Class Favorite" or something similar. Everyone knew who I was, and I was fairly well liked, but now I realize that many things I did were only attempts to attract and win friends. Although I loved cheerleading, I remember almost quitting the squad one year because cheerleading was not the cool thing to do; basketball was what everyone wanted to play that year. I tried to wear things that were in style and hang around cool kids. I wanted to associate with them so that I too could be a part of the crowd that everyone liked. Most of the time, I didn't fit in with that crowd. They were often involved in things that I didn't do. However, I was determined to be liked and wanted to do whatever it took to make that happen, even if it meant letting some of my standards slide.

Others would often tease me harshly in front of a crowd when my drastic attempts to fit in fell short. I found in the end that my efforts were all in vain. I discovered that it is impossible to fit in and be liked by everyone else when you choose to walk a certain path. The Bible says that we are aliens and strangers in this world and that we are indeed a very peculiar people (1 Peter 2:11). We are supposed to be holy and set apart in every aspect of our lives. We are not supposed to look like the world by any means. We should . . .

talk differently

walk differently

work differently

eat differently

play differently

parent differently

spend differently

live differently!

Our transformed lives should sharply contrast with the lives of those around us who are ungodly. Since God calls us to a higher standard of living, it is impossible to follow those who choose to conform.

It will be hard when you see your co-workers acting unethically and seemingly getting away with it. It will be difficult when your single friends who live immorally are marrying great guys. The trip to Judah will seem worthless when you are the only one who has chosen this route. It is a straight and narrow road that leads to Judah as opposed to a wide highway that leads to Moab. You must determine in your heart

It is a straight and narrow road that leads to Judah as opposed to a wide highway that leads to Moab.

that, regardless of what others choose to do, you will continue to press on toward Judah. The reward for your faithfulness is waiting there.

When a young couple was in their first years of marriage, the twenty-five-year-old husband worked hard to take care of his family financially while also going to school full time to get his graduate degree. It was an extremely difficult task, but he was very persistent. He brought home only $300 per month to feed and clothe his wife and two baby girls, working through the night at a bus station unloading passenger buses. However, since there was little traffic at night and some buses came in with no passengers, this was very tedious, boring work.

The other young men with whom he worked came up with a scheme to ease the boredom and help each other get some rest. Some workers would stay home and come into work late while the other guys would punch in their time cards for them. This way they would still be getting their full paychecks without having to sit through long, sleepy nights at work. Other nights, the guys would punch in and then take shifts sleeping while the others covered for them. This would often leave the young husband and father alone to unpack the buses by himself. On many occasions, the other men invited him to join them in this seemingly successful scam. He always turned them down. He was the only worker who would punch in his time card honestly and stay awake during his shift. This was difficult, and I wonder if I would have been able to do the same. But he was consistent and faithful in his job, and he maintained his integrity.

One day the young man's supervisor called him into the office.

The supervisor said, "For the last several months I have been sending a 'mystery passenger' into the bus station in the middle of the night in order to keep an eye on the workers and the events at the bus station." The mystery passenger had become aware of the scam that the co-workers were running and had conveyed everything to the supervisor.

At the same time, the mystery passenger also informed the supervisor that while others were asleep on the job or not even present, one particular young man had been hard at work every night without fail. The supervisor commended the young man for his hard work and especially for his integrity—that he was doing what was right when he thought no one was watching. Then the boss promoted him to night shift manager, making much more money than he could have imagined! He was now supervising the young men who had been his peers.

How glad I am that my dad, the young man in this story, decided to do what was right those years working at the bus station. He pressed on to Judah even when everyone else had decided that the easiest route was back to Moab. I thank the Lord for this legacy of godliness my father has given to me.

No Turning Back

Comfort through conformity may be in Moab, but the favor of God is in Judah!

Remember, you can go back to Moab and all that it represents if you choose. God will never force you to continue the journey to Judah. And when you return to your old way of living, you may feel comfortable. You may obtain some of the longing of your heart. When you go back to conforming to what everyone else wants for your life, no one will harass you anymore. Comfort through conformity may be in Moab, but the favor of God is in Judah! Orpah was probably very comfortable and content in Moab. She probably felt very good about her decision to return. I am certain that seeing the faces of her family members and friends was very soothing for her. But while Orpah was finding comfort, Ruth was finding the peace of God despite her discomfort. She was finding favor, miraculous blessing, and abundant grace right from the throne of the God of Israel.

The Bible says in Galatians 5:17 that the flesh and the spirit are at war against each other, and both are battling to win you over. Please be aware that this is by no means fun and games. This is war! Your flesh wants to resist the path you take to continue to Judah and follow God; it will work against you every step of the way. This battle over your decision to continue or go back is no walk in the park. Rather, it is a bitter fight to the very end. Although once you are saved, your soul can never be won back from the hands of our great God, to compromise victory in this earthly battle can steal your joy and cause great pain in this life. *Do not take this battle lightly.* The flesh wants you all to itself, and so does the Spirit. Both are battling for control over you.

This battle becomes more evident to us when we are at the moment of decision. Will we choose to turn around and walk back to the city that God delivered us from, or will we continue to press toward the calling of God? When we encounter the Lord, we should be willing to choose a different path than we may have chosen last year, last month, or even this time yesterday. Although Ruth's circumstances were devastating, she chose a different path than her sister-in-law. She chose the favor of God over comfort, God's blessings over her own desires, and conformity to God rather than to the world. Will you?

CHAPTER TWELVE

A Different
ATTITUDE

ORPAH AND RUTH were torn between their desire to return to familiarity and their commitment to stay with their mother-in-law whom they loved dearly. The internal struggle of these women became externally apparent as, two separate times, they wept uncontrollably. It seems as if both were prepared to do what was right in the eyes of the Lord. Their tears suggested that they were spiritually in tune with what would honor their mother-in-law and God in this situation. They *both* looked the part, but only *one* of them was the real deal!

After the second round of tears in Ruth 1:14, "Orpah kissed her mother-in-law good-by, but Ruth clung to her." With tears in their eyes, both of them looked like women of commitment and women of their word. However, when it came down to it, Orpah turned back. In the end, she really couldn't leave all of the lures of Moab behind for the unknown of Judah. Orpah, despite her tears, didn't have the inner commitment to match her external promises. Her initial efforts implied that she had left behind the gods of Moab, when in reality she was still clinging to the comfort and familiarity of her gods and what they stood for. An encounter with God reveals who is and who isn't serious about following Him. And for those who are serious, the encounter changes their attitude about what it means to follow Him.

Pleasing God Alone

I believe we have a generation of Christians today who are just good performers. We look the part but aren't really who we claim to be. We are Oscar-winning Christian actors and actresses. We have our lines well memorized. The only problem is that there is nothing inside backing up all our talk. We are just good at playing the game. We are imposters and hypocrites, and as a result, we disgrace the kingdom of God. The Lord's desire is that we not "play" Christian anymore. He wants us to devote ourselves to Him, not because someone else is watching, not because we want to entertain, not because we have a desire to impress, but only because we want to please Him.

I have to preface this story by telling you that my dad is the most . . . how do I say it . . . *domestically challenged* person I have ever met! He doesn't do dishes or wash clothes. He is not a good cook and isn't interested in making beds or dusting furniture. Not only is he not interested—he doesn't know *how* to do those things. In other words, he really needs my mom to survive! When I was single, I thought all marriages operated this way. I assumed that most men really *needed* their wives to take care of them, just like my dad did. So, going into marriage, I assumed that my future mate would be so fortunate to have me because I would be the Martha Stewart of his existence and impress him so much. Boy, was *I* in for a surprise!

My husband's parents reared him in a military family and trained him to do chores. There were hospital corners on beds and perfectly folded clothes in closets in his home. Little did I know that I had married Chef Boyardee! Jerry also happens to be an amazing cook and quite competent at cleaning, but I didn't fully discover this until we went on our first grocery shopping trip together soon after we married. Not a good idea!

At the grocery store, I was certain that I was going to teach him a thing or two about shopping! The first aisle we walked down was the water aisle. He turned to me and said, "Honey, which type of drinking water would you prefer?" I looked at him with a quizzical expression and said, "The cheap kind." He went on to explain to me why the cheap kind wasn't necessarily the best or best-tasting kind. To me, water was water.

The next aisle we shopped was the cleaning aisle. He turned to me and asked which type of bathroom and kitchen cleaner I would prefer to use. The fact that he even cared mesmerized me! I suggested, "Well, 409® cleans everything, doesn't it?" He laughed a little and explained to me that *certain* cleaners were only good for some things, and other cleaners were better used elsewhere. I couldn't believe it. This man knew everything! Don't get me started on what happened at the deli counter!

I was very disheartened by all of this. My husband knew more about grocery shopping than I did, and it horrified me. He would even refold the clothes that I had folded for him, according to his specifications. One day I came home to find my husband making a peach cobbler—from scratch! I wouldn't even know where to start from scratch!

I was so discouraged by all of this that I called my mama! I told her my problem, and after listening to my sob story, she said to me what you might be thinking right now, "Girl, you'd better put your feet up on the couch and let that man cook and clean!" She went on to explain that this was just a small matter and that I should not let it interrupt the grand scheme of our relationship. In fact, she cautioned me to remember that what mattered most was our commitment and love.

Jesus wants us to focus on our love relationship with him and not be so busy trying to perform for Him.

I vowed that day to remember that Jerry did not love me because of what I once thought were my amazing domestic qualities. I did not have to impress him. Jerry loves me for *me*. In the same way, Jesus wants us to focus on our love relationship with him and not be so busy trying to perform for Him that we forget to relax in His love.

This is a continual struggle for me and for those who find themselves in a position where people are watching. I have to call on the Lord daily to help me remember that He is the only One who must be pleased with my service to Him. You see, the crowds can applaud, the auditoriums can be filled to capacity, the onlookers can smile with enthusiasm, and the readers can even ask for my signature inside my latest book. However, if God is not applauding, if God is not the true audience, if God is not smiling and pleased with the material that I write, then all has been in vain.

I want to please the Lord with my ministry by living a lifestyle that validates my message. I want Him to applaud the words I say and write because He knows that they come out of a deep-rooted relationship that supersedes any earthly accolades. My desire should be only to please the Lord.

Matthew 6:1 says, "Be careful not to do your 'acts of righteousness' before men, to be seen by them. If you do, you will have no reward from your Father in heaven." If you and I enjoy human applause now, we had better milk it for all it's worth, because that is all we will ever get! That doesn't mean that you can't accept any appreciation and accolades that you may receive for whatever you do, but do not do those works with the deliberate intention of winning awards and recognition. I don't know about you, but I will gladly trade the appreciation others may give in order to make my Savior happy.

Anne Graham Lotz, the daughter of Billy Graham, once said to me, "Priscilla, so many people who have big ministries and big followings will get to heaven and find out that they weren't even on the front lines. I just want to be on the front lines."

Where are these front lines? They're on the playing fields of our faith, just on different yard lines. Some have been called to the fifty-yard line—the place the crowds consider to be mediocre. Not necessarily close to a touchdown in either direction but still on the field of play. How often I have met homemakers whose ministry is to their children, an extremely important ministry indeed, yet they feel sedentary and useless on this yard line. God has given them this field position, but it is hard for them to accept it. God has given others a position so close to the end zone that everyone notices their victories. Everyone cheers and celebrates their expressive gifts or talents. This is their front line. What matters most is not the yard line on which God places you, but whether you make the most of your position for the glory of the Most High King.

For His Glory

"The people did not come to see me. They came to see God."

—Elisabeth Elliot

One of my favorite Bible teachers, Elisabeth Elliot, was once questioned by a young woman about her rather dry, straightforward presentations. The woman asked why she chose not to use jokes and stories in her speeches. Why was it that she always just jumped right to the message without feeling the need to "warm up the audience" as many speakers often do? Her answer should be the sentiment of all of our hearts: "The people did not come to see me. They came to see God."

In our work for the Lord, we must thoroughly question our motives and separate the righteous from the unrighteous so that we are following His desires and not our own. Whether we serve God from the pulpit or the pew, through mass media or as a member of a small Bible study group, our motto must be "The people did not come to see me. They came to see God."

In many of our Christian circles, serving Christ is in fashion right now, so we must take inventory of our motives. What is the real reason why we do what we do? Whether our calling has been to the masses or just to our neighbors, to the church family or to our own family, we must be careful to evaluate the motive behind our service. Are we serving Him for His glory or for our own? Is our goal to turn eyes to Him or eyes toward ourselves? Who is our focus?

I have read stories of missionaries and great servants of God who worked for Him without complaint yet under unbelievably strenuous conditions. I have read about many martyrs who chose to serve Him in the face of adversity and great danger. These saints were forced to choose between their lives and the gospel; yet, for some of us, our hardest choice is whether or not to fly first class to our next "work project for the Lord." While we are so concerned about our personal comfort, other believers lived in horrendous conditions, suffered the death of fellow workers, went without food, and were exposed to life-threatening diseases, yet they remained focused on the reason for their mission.

Why? Because their focus was not on their well-being and their earthly awards; their only concern was God's receiving the glory for the work that He sent them to do. How often have we found ourselves disgruntled if the hotel accommodations on our mission trip are not what we expected! We all need to evaluate the reason for our service. If we are serving for the Savior and for Him alone, then we must go away "rejoicing because [we have] been counted worthy of suffering disgrace for the Name" (Acts 5:41).

Our attitude should be one of willingness to accept any negative circumstances that may come our way while expressing gratitude that

God would use us in the midst of them. Paul said in Philippians 2:5–7: "Your attitude should be the same as that of Christ Jesus: Who, being in very nature God, did not consider equality with God something to be grasped, but made himself nothing, taking the very nature of a servant, being made in human likeness." Paul's message is clear. Jesus,

the One who is the Christ

the One who rules over the earth and heavens

the One who created everything therein

the One who deserves the highest worship and praise

the One who has always been and always will be

the One who is the embodiment of the Word

the One who is Lord of all

the One who is most beloved of the Father

the One whose kingdom shall never end

the One at whose name every knee will bow

the One at whose name every tongue will confess

the One who heals our iniquities and sins

the One whose very name causes hell and all its demons to shudder . . .

. . . *this Jesus* alone is the One who had the right to demand the respect that He so obviously deserved while He was on earth. However, Jesus emptied Himself so that He could properly serve His Father. Unlike Jesus, we are often so *full* of ourselves that there is no room left for the true service and worship of the One who really deserves it! We have all fallen victim to this frailty of our humanity, and I certainly am no exception.

One of my favorite singing groups recently ended after thirty-one years of music ministry. *Truth* was a dynamic singing group who ministered across the country and abroad. My brother, Anthony, to whom I dedicated this book, traveled and sang with them for two years. During this time, I learned more about their ministry and gained a great respect for their faithfulness. In the two years that Anthony participated, they did 520 concerts! The men who performed also gave an extra two hours to set up and two hours to tear down the stage, including the lights, microphones, and heavy sound equipment, every single performance night. These young men and women gave up all semblance of a normal life to travel by bus from city to city and spread the gospel through song for a year or more of their lives.

Effective disciples must be empty disciples.

The most incredible part about this is that these young people did all of this for about $50 a week. Surely, their incredible singing voices could have earned them high dollars elsewhere, yet they chose to forgo monetary gain in order to serve the Lord in this capacity. They were a constant reminder to me to check my motives in ministry and in my service to God. These talented people had to empty themselves every moment of every day. There was no room on their small bus for people who were full of themselves! Effective disciples must be empty disciples.

When Jerry and I started talking about getting married, I suddenly became infatuated with diamonds. I wanted to know everything and was attracted to any store that had anything to do with them. One store I discovered in the Galleria mall in Dallas always had its front windows laden with incredible stones. There were rubies, sapphires, and incredible diamonds. I was in diamond wonderland! On my first visit to the store, I gawked in the window for a while before finally entering the store. The diamonds that I found inside were even more incredible than those I had seen in the window.

One in particular captured my attention. It was stunning! After staring at it longingly, I asked the clerk if he could take it out of the glass case so I could have a better look at it. Now this diamond was *big!* I knew there was no way that we could afford it, but I wanted to just indulge myself in a fantasy and see it anyway. The clerk took it out of the case and laid it on the counter on a black velvet cloth. He brought over a light to shine on the merchandise, and it glistened brilliantly. I was mesmerized. I took my time peering down at this masterpiece and slowly lifted my head and asked, "How much does this diamond cost?"

The clerk replied, "Twenty-nine dollars and ninety-five cents."

I just stood there for a moment, stunned, before what he told me sank in. Naturally, I then replied, "I'll take four!"

This diamond was so cheap because it wasn't a diamond at all. It was a cubic zirconium shaped and cut to look like the real thing. However, if you were to cut deep into this stone or test it, you would easily discover that it was only glass.

Some of us are just like that pseudo diamond. We look like the real thing, but when we are tested by tough situations and laid open before the Father, we prove to be only an imitation. We have an outer spiritual shell that performs well under slight pressure. We are always at church and we are even involved in ministry, but we only look the part. There is nothing of substance internally to validate what we say. We are simply on display. An encounter with God should change that. When we see Him for who He really is and see the evidence of His handiwork in our lives, we should no longer operate as imitations. Our actions should be pure and holy before the Lord—an acceptable offering to Him.

Chuck Swindoll once told a story of a young man who was taking a journey on foot. During his journey, he came to an enormous body of water. Standing on the shore, he saw nothing but water in front of him. The water loudly rushing across the rocks intimidated him as he contemplated his options. He finally decided that the only way to get to his destination was to try to go right through the middle of it. He took a step into the water, and right at the shoreline it was only two inches deep. He took another step, and the water was only two inches deep. In fact, he continued all the way across this rushing body of water, and it never got any deeper than two inches.

Some of our lives are like that body of water. We make so much spiritual clamor that we are very intimidating, but when people take a step into our lives, they find out that we are only two inches deep. What a tragedy it would be for us to look the part but not have the spiritual depth to match! That is what the Lord wants for us—to make us a lot deeper than we are wide so He can really use us in His plans. I pray constantly for myself and others in this area. It can become so easy to play the role of Christian for an entire lifetime and not ever truly know Him and the abundant life that He desires to give.

> *All trials and tribulations in our lives fall into one of two categories: either God-sent or God-allowed.*

The Triumph of Our Trials

Ruth's transformation took place against a backdrop of tragedy and pain, and her greatest triumph came through trial. Please remember that the period of turmoil your life may be in right now could be God's tool to help you to go deeper in Him. "The testing of your faith develops perseverance" (James 1:3).

All trials and tribulations in our lives fall into one of two categories: either God-sent or God-allowed. Either way, God will use that trial for your good. In Ruth's case, God used her trial to fulfill a greater purpose beyond her wildest dreams. And in the process, she and Orpah discovered truths about themselves that they may not have known before. If you find yourself in the middle of a dark situation in your life right now, don't be dismayed. God is not shocked at what is happening in your life. He is using it to work toward His goal in your life and to make you into what He desires you to be.

Jeffrey Johnson, a pastor and anointed minister of the Word of God, thoroughly challenged me with a message that he delivered at our church recently. He said that sometimes we see the trying situations in our lives as the devil's attempt to push us off course. Pastor Johnson reminded us that sometimes the Lord shakes up our situations in order to cause us to produce things that we never thought possible. In Haggai 2:21–22, God says, "I will shake the heavens and the earth. I will overturn royal thrones and shatter the power of the foreign kingdoms. I will overthrow chariots and their drivers; horses and their riders will fall." In this instance, the Lord said that things are going to be shaken up, and He is going to be the One doing the shaking!

If your situation is a little shaky right now, the Lord could be behind it. Don't necessarily blame your problem on the devil. Pastor Johnson told about the old pink piggy bank with the coin slot on top that he had when he was young. He said that he would sometimes turn his piggy bank upside down and begin to shake it. Why? He wanted something of value on the inside.

If God is doing the shaking in your life, His goal is to shake something of value out of you. God will shake you and me until He gets exactly what He is looking for out of us. He knows how much value you have in you, because He is the One who has been investing in you all this time. He will shake and shake until you produce precious treasure for His kingdom. He wants it to be produced from the inside out, though. He doesn't want a show. He wants to see the real value that is deep inside of you. No more imposters!

He is the only thing that does not change in a world that is always changing.

The Unchanging God

While Orpah was turning back to Moab, Ruth was proclaiming her complete reliance on and commitment to her God. She said to Naomi, "Don't urge me to leave you or to turn back from you. Where you go I will go, and where you stay I will stay. Your people will be my people and your God my God" (Ruth 1:16).

At the end of it all, you and I have to be committed to God and God alone. He is the only thing that does not change in a world that is always changing. He is the only true constant in your life.

Your husband will change.

Your children will change.

Your friends will change.

Your career will change.

Your neighborhood will change.

Your bank account balance will change.

Your portfolio will change.

You will change.

In fact, your entire life can be turned upside down in just an instant! Yet in spite of all of that,

He will still be sitting on the throne.

He will still be in control of this world.

He will still be overseeing the furthest reaches of the universe.

He will still be watching over you.

He will still own the cattle on a thousand hills.

He will still be King of kings and Lord of lords!

Like Ruth, we must bank our bottom dollar only on Him. We must get so serious about our commitment to Him that we don't have to put on a show anymore. Any emotion we show, any good deed that we do, any spectacle that we parade will not have its roots in getting attention or receiving applause. It will be designed only to be offered to the One to whom we have committed our lives. Every tear shed, speech given, song sung, ministry led, thirst quenched, or hunger fed will not be done for our own glory but only for the glory of the Lord.

CHAPTER THIRTEEN

From the Mediocre to the MIRACULOUS

RUTH HAD NO IDEA what the outcome of her choice to follow God's path alongside her mother-in-law would be. However, I can imagine that from her perspective, it looked bleak. She probably envisioned being lonely the rest of her life, because she would likely never marry again. It had been a fluke the first time, so surely it wouldn't happen a second time. She would have to live with Jewish people who had no regard for pagans like her. Even so, she knew that what she was doing was right in God's eyes, and somehow He would bring something miraculous about in her life. We cannot expect to receive the miraculous things of God without being utterly committed to obedience.

Transformation Requires Obedience

Ephesians 3:20 declares that He will do well beyond what we can ask or even imagine, but it is only "according to his power that is at work within us." In other words, if there is no power inwardly, there will be no benefits outwardly. You and I must obey, no matter what the cost seems to be. Obedience sets the stage for His power. We must know the

Word of the Lord and let it saturate our minds so we can practically apply it to our lives.

My father doesn't know how to type or use a computer at all. To this day, he still prepares for sermons by handwriting all of his notes on a yellow legal pad. He has never even sent an e-mail. He hates computers! However, he recently wanted to go online to find my brother Jonathan on the website for Baylor University, where he plays football. He asked my sister Chrystal for help, and she showed him how to turn the computer on (they were really starting from scratch here!), log onto the Internet, type in the university's URL address, and find the web page. After finding the site for him, my sister ran to answer the telephone. Right before she left the room, Dad yelled out, "How do I maneuver my way around this page so that I can find Jonathan?"

She answered loudly, "Use the mouse!"

Moments later she returned to a very disturbing sight. There sat my father with the mouse in his hand, waving it around in midair. She watched him for a few moments in complete shock. When he saw no results from waving the mouse, he then put it flat against the computer screen and moved it up, down, and side to side. He even got irritated that the thing wasn't working!

My sister almost died laughing that a man as smart as my dad didn't know that the mouse was supposed to stay flat on the desk. She couldn't believe that anyone on the planet could be that computer illiterate! My dad has a computer at the house and a laptop that sits in a drawer in his office. He has access to these pieces of equipment, but he doesn't know how to use them. What good is a computer if you don't know how to use it?

What good is the Bible if you and I don't learn how to use it? In order to benefit from all that the Word has to offer and to receive the promises it outlines for our lives, we have to be ready to play by the rulebook. We can't wave the Bible around and expect to see results. We

The benefits of following Christ directly relate to His lordship over your life.

have to know the Word and apply it to our lives in order to experience its benefits. We can talk about obedience all day, but the Bible is our manual on *how* to be obedient.

The benefits of following Christ directly relate to His lordship over your life. For example, the Bible says that "he will give you the desires of your heart." However, that doesn't mean He will grant any desires. What precedes that promise is a command to "delight yourself in the Lord" (Psalm 37:4). Scripture gives us many if/then statements: *If* you are obedient, *then* you will receive a blessing. Here are just a few more examples:

Humble yourselves, therefore, under God's mighty hand, that he may lift you up in due time (1 Peter 5:6).

Commit your way to the LORD; trust in him and he will do this: He will make your righteousness shine like the dawn, the justice of your cause like the noonday sun (Psalm 37:5–6).

Come near to God and he will come near to you (James 4:8).

Wait for the LORD and keep his way. He will exalt you to inherit the land; when the wicked are cut off, you will see it (Psalm 37:34).

Submit yourselves, then, to God. Resist the devil, and he will flee from you (James 4:7).

Turn from evil and do good; then you will dwell in the land forever (Psalm 37:27).

All these blessings will come upon you and accompany you if you obey the LORD your God (Deuteronomy 28:2).

In fact, the entire chapter of Deuteronomy 28 declares many extravagant blessings over your life and promises the wondrous outcome of your situation, but only "if you fully obey the LORD your God and carefully follow all his commands" (28:1). If you and I choose obedience over disobedience, then all of God's blessings will be showered upon us. To receive the promises of God, we must be obedient; to be obedient, we must know the Word of God and submit ourselves to it.

> *In order to benefit from the Word of God, you and I have to put it on.*

On a recent walk with my friend Michelle in the chilly winter air, we tucked our chins and hunched our shoulders with a shiver when the temperature dropped suddenly. Michelle had a jacket with her, but she was holding it in her hands. She kept complaining about the cold, but she didn't want to take the time and energy to put on her jacket! What good could the jacket do her if she refused to put it on? In order to benefit from the Word of God, you and I have to put it on. You cannot just hold it nearby and think that you will not freeze in the cold climate of the world. You have to get the Word out of your hands and "put it on" in your heart. It must become a way of life. Then you will find shelter from the cold.

This is what Ruth did. She knew the truth because Naomi had likely told her all the stories of God's faithfulness. She rehearsed His faithfulness in her mind, she meditated on the things Naomi taught her about obeying God, and then she put it into practice in her daily lifestyle. Although Ruth did not have the written Testaments that you and I have today, she followed the precepts of God that she had heard from Naomi.

Ephesians 6:13 says this: "Put on the full armor of God, so that when the day of evil comes, you may be able to stand your ground, and after you have done everything, to stand." Putting on the Word is a conscious decision and deliberate choice you must make every day. You must choose to . . .

Buckle the belt of truth around your waist.

Put on the breastplate of righteousness.

Prepare your feet with the readiness of the gospel of peace.

Take up the shield of faith.

Put on the helmet of salvation.

And take the sword of the Spirit (see Ephesians 6:14–17).

God's Sovereignty

When Ruth arrived in Bethlehem, she got busy right away. She went to glean in a field in order to provide food for herself and her mother-in-law. In one of the clearest examples of the sovereignty of God recorded in the Bible, Ruth "happened" to begin working in a field that was owned by a man named Boaz—a well-respected relative of Naomi's.

The sovereignty of God can keep you sane and peaceful in the midst of nightmarish circumstances. Knowing that He is in control of everyone and everything can keep you from looking over your shoulder, living in fear, losing your integrity, or worrying about the future. When you and I encounter His sovereignty, then we understand that the outcome of our circumstances is under the control of the Mighty One. What peace comes from knowing that He is still on the throne, regardless of the dealings of this world. "'For I know the plans I have for you,' declares the LORD, 'plans to prosper you and not to harm you, plans to give you hope and a future'" (Jeremiah 29:11).

In His undying love for you, He has declared that your future will be full of hope. Don't worry about the outcome; that is not up to you. The most you can do is worry yourself into an early grave. The outcome is in the hands of the Master. You and I must simply be obedient and trust Him for the rest.

Jehovah-Jireh, My Provider

In chapters 2—4 of Ruth, when Boaz discovered who Ruth was, what she had done for Naomi, and what she chose to sacrifice by leaving Moab, he determined to fulfill the role of a kinsman-redeemer. In ancient times, the kinsman-redeemer, usually the closest relative of the widow's husband, was the one who provided for the needs of the widow and her family. According to the law, Ruth could marry a brother of her dead husband. This man would become the kinsman-redeemer. However, since both Naomi's sons were dead, this role fell to the next closest relative. In this case, that close relative relinquished his right to marry Ruth, and the responsibility fell to Boaz, who was next in line. As Ruth's kinsman-redeemer, he decided to do two things for this woman—the same things that Jesus will do for you.

Boaz determined immediately that he would be Ruth's provider. In Ruth 2:8–9, he said, "Don't go and glean in another field and don't go away from here. Stay here with my servant girls. Watch the field where the men are harvesting, and follow along after the girls. I have told the men not to touch you. And whenever you are thirsty, go and get a drink from the water jars the men have filled." As they worked, reapers always left extra barley for the poor to pick up for themselves. However, Boaz went so far as to let Ruth have as much as she wanted without any opposition from the workers. He gave her water to quench her thirst and rest to soothe her spirit.

Boaz anticipated her need for rest and water and provided a place for those needs to be met. In the same way, Jesus, the Living Water, will quench our spiritual thirst (John 4) and provide rest for those who come to Him (Matthew 11:28). He has anticipated our need for refreshment and has provided an abundant, overflowing, never-ending supply of water in Himself. Do you need grace, mercy, peace, hope, and joy in your journey? He is all of these things. Don't go to everything else to quench your thirst—just come to Him! He is constantly ready to quench your spiritual thirst. Come to the Fountain that will never run dry.

When you determine to stay committed to the Lord, no matter what the cost, you too will have the favor of Jesus, your heavenly Kinsman-redeemer. He might decide not to take you out of your uncomfortable situation, but He will alleviate some of the difficulty of it. He may not remove you from the storm, but He will give you unfathomable peace in the midst of it.

"And the peace of God, which transcends all understanding, will guard your hearts and your minds in Christ Jesus" (Philippians 4:7).

Like Ruth, we do not have to be crushed by situations that would crush the normal human. We do not have to be discouraged to the point of depression or emotional breakdowns. We have a Kinsman-redeemer who is with us and who is determined to give us peace in the midst of the storm. Through His grace, He will make our lives easier while we are still on the job, gleaning in the field where He's placed us.

Yet, Boaz didn't stop there in his provision for Ruth. "At mealtime Boaz said to her, 'Come over here. Have some bread and dip it in the wine vinegar.' When she sat down with the harvesters, he offered her some roasted grain. She ate all she wanted and had some left over" (Ruth 2:14). Oh, I love this. It is so incredible! After easing the heavy load of her burden and quenching her physical thirst, he now extends an invitation to dinner.

From Ruth's perspective, there is a problem here. She is a foreign woman and the reapers are Jews. However, the boss has invited her to the table as a V.I.P.—and the boss himself soon served her roasted grain in the midst of them all! In the same way, Jesus prepares a table for us in the presence of our enemies (Psalm 23:5). You will eat from the hand of the Master in the presence of those who ridicule and persecute you. He will come and serve you personally. The outcome of your situation includes a dinner invitation from the King and a V.I.P. seat at His table.

Better yet, the blessings of God are not simply satisfying; they are excessive! They are more than you can contain. Not only does He provide for our needs, but He provides so generously that our cup over-flows. Ruth not only had enough to eat but she even had some to take home to Naomi (Ruth 2:18). When the Lord blesses you and invites you to His table, there will be enough for you to share with others! The miraculous future in store for you and the outcome of your circum-stances include the provision of the King of kings and Lord of lords.

Jehovah-Magen, My Protection

Boaz was not only Ruth's provision; he was also her protection. Three times in Ruth 2 he tells his servants not to touch her or insult her or rebuke her. Boaz went to those who could have caused Ruth hurt and shame and commanded them to leave her alone. Of this passage, Matthew Henry writes in his commentary on Ruth, "He charged all his servants to be very tender of her and respectful to her, and no doubt they would be so to one to whom they saw their master kind. She was a stranger, and it is probable her language, dress, and mien differed much from theirs; but he charged them that they should not in any thing affront her, or be abusive to her, as rude servants are too apt to be to strangers."

If Jesus is the One who has gone before you and has declared your protection, then you cannot be harmed.

Boaz, her kinsman-redeemer, became her protector. He offered a place of refuge for her in the midst of a trying situation. Jesus does the same for us. It does not matter how formidable your situation looks at home or at work. If Jesus is the One who has gone before you and has declared your protection, then you cannot be harmed. The hedge of protection that He has built around you cannot be torn down or even disturbed. He is Boss, and when He declares that something is so, it is so! You are divinely protected. Psalms 105:15 says, "Do not touch my anointed ones; do my prophets no harm." Are you afraid for your safety today? The wondrous outcome of your circumstances includes the divine protection of an all-powerful Savior.

The protection the Lord offers you is the most secure available. It doesn't matter how many bars you put on your windows or how expensive your home alarm system is. It is irrelevant how hidden your safety deposit box is from public view or how big the dogs are that guard your property. "Unless the LORD watches over the city, the watchmen stand guard in vain" (Psalm 127:1). The best protection in the universe has been granted to you as a daughter of the King.

In 1988, a series of forest fires ravaged Yellowstone National Park. One fire was utterly unstoppable, and the firefighters could do nothing but wait for it to burn itself out. Afterward, the forest rangers searched through the burned wasteland to salvage anything they could. One of the rangers came across a sight that sickened him. Standing like a statue was a dead bird that had been burned to a crisp in the fire. He tipped over the carcass with his foot. To his amazement, out from underneath the dead bird scampered five little baby birds. They were living under the protective wings of their mother. That mother bird had stood in the fire and burned to death to protect her babies, who were unable to fly to safety.

Jesus has provided a refuge for you in the midst of seemingly hopeless circumstances. In Ruth 2:12, Boaz says to Ruth, "May the LORD repay you for what you have done. May you be richly rewarded by the LORD, the God of Israel, under whose wings you have come to take refuge." Likewise, Psalm 91:4 says, "He will cover you with his feathers, and under his wings you will find refuge; his faithfulness will be your shield and rampart." Come under His strong wings, and find protection there. He is your only true refuge, and like the mother bird in Yellowstone, Jesus has intentionally and lovingly suffered pain, torture, and death to protect His precious babies. Rest under the wings of your God.

The Miracle of Transformation

After Ruth met Boaz and accepted his selfless love and commitment, they wed. Then "the LORD enabled her to conceive, and she gave birth to a son" (Ruth 4:13). Now she had received redemption and the favor of God both in her marriage and in her womb.

Little did she know that she and her son would be used mightily in the kingdom of God. Ruth 4:17 explains, "And they named him Obed. He was the father of Jesse, the father of David." In other words Ruth, the poor widow from a pagan nation, was the great King David's great-grandmother! And of course, David's direct descendent was Jesus, the Messiah. Even today, the ripple effect of her transformation from the mediocre to the miraculous has touched hundreds of thousands of generations. She is an ancestor of the Lamb of God, sent to save the world from their sins! When we encounter God, our miracle of transformation has the ability to touch many lives for His sake and for His glory.

"He that forsakes all for Christ shall find more than all with him; it shall be recompensed a hundred-fold in this present time."

—Matthew Henry

Her despair and discomfort during those tumultuous years were necessary to move Ruth into a position where God could be glorified and His kingdom could come. Her hard times were not about her at all. They were purely designed for the glory of God! They happened so that you and I could live in the freedom of Christ's salvation in the twenty-first century! Ruth was committed, willing, and obedient, and as a result, her legacy produced the Savior of the world. The outcome of her circumstance was beyond miraculous!

If God can use a woman who was grief-stricken, displaced, destitute, and seemingly hopeless to be the ancestor of the holy Messiah, then He can also use you and me. We must simply be willing to yield to Him and be changed by grace. Maybe what the Lord is doing in your life right now isn't about you. Have you ever considered that what God is orchestrating might be for the benefit of those who will follow you? Your obedience is required today so that your miraculous outcome can bless both you and those who benefit from your life tomorrow.

Step to the
EDGE

EVEN AFTER WE HAVE encountered God, the prospect of making drastic changes in our lives may feel intimidating. When we consider the opportunities to exercise our faith and take a stand, we may feel a wave of the same fear and uncertainty as we did before we first encountered God. Making the decision to change is a scary thing . . . especially when the consequences are largely unknown. We know we must change, but what will that be like?

"My child,

trust Me and go

to the edge."

It is as if a daunting precipice is in front of us and beyond it an intimidating darkness. The precipice looks dangerous and risky. Yet when we come to the cliff's edge of decision in our lives, that's when God usually says in a still quiet voice, "My child, trust me and go to the edge."

And we say, "But, God, have You seen how far it is down there? Surely You don't want me to go to that edge!"

And He says again, "My child, you can go to the edge."

"But God," we clamor, "I am far more comfortable here than if I went to the edge of that cliff. I know that You can't mean that You want me to go to this edge. Surely I am hearing Your voice wrong."

He says, "No, my child, you heard correctly. Trust Me and go to the edge."

Just about the time we get up the courage to go right up to the edge of change . . . He pushes us off and into the unknown! Then, and not a moment too soon, we spread wings that we never knew we had, and we fly. Like a caterpillar transformed into a beautiful winged butter-fly, we soar over our circumstances in a way that we never thought we could. We realize how much we have changed and how good our trans-formation feels. We would have never known our potential unless we went, despite our fear, to the edge, and His loving hand prompted us to fly.

Be encouraged, my friend! Go ahead and step to the edge! The sooner you do, the sooner you will experience the gift of an encounter with a transforming God.

TO CONTACT THE AUTHOR:

Priscilla Shirer

The Shirer Group

P.O. Box 2122

Cedar Hill, Texas 75106-2122

(214) 467-3382

www.priscillaspeaks.com

A Jewel In His Crown

Rediscovering Your Value As a Woman of Excellence

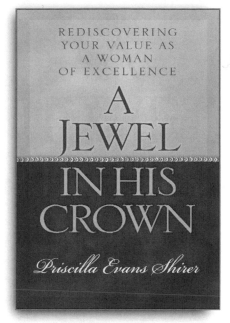

ISBN: 0-8024-4097-5

When they become weary and discouraged, women lose sight of their real value as beloved daughters of God. *A Jewel in His Crown* examines how the way women view their worth deeply affects their relationships. This book teaches women how to renew strength and be women of excellence.

Priscilla Shirer herself is a crown jewel, mined from a family of precious gems. Reading her book is like a walk through Tiffany's as she uses her insight to draw the readers attention to the various facets of a godly woman's character. My prayer is that God will use A Jewel in His Crown *to help women embrace their primary aim of brining glory to God through the uniqueness of who they are in Christ.*

Anne Graham Lotz, AnGel Ministries

MOODY
PUBLISHERS

THE NAME YOU CAN TRUST•

1-800-678-6928 www.MoodyPublishers.com

AND WE ARE CHANGED TEAM

ACQUIRING EDITOR:
Elsa Mazon

COPY EDITOR:
The Livingstone Corporation

BACK COVER COPY:
The Livingstone Corporation

COVER DESIGN:
Ragont Design

INTERIOR DESIGN:
The Livingstone Corporation

PRINTING AND BINDING:
Versa Press Inc.